Career Launcher

Nonprofit
Organizations

Career Launcher series

Advertising and Public Relations
Computers and Programming
Education
Energy
Fashion
Film
Finance
Food Services
Hospitality
Internet
Health Care Management
Health Care Providers
Law
Law Enforcement and Public Safety
Manufacturing
Nonprofit Organizations
Performing Arts
Professional Sports Organizations
Real Estate
Recording Industry
Television
Video Games

Career Launcher

Nonprofit
Organizations

Ann Morrill

Ferguson Publishing
An imprint of Infobase Publishing

Ferguson
An imprint of Infobase Publishing
132 West 31st Street
New York NY 10001

Library of Congress Cataloging-in-Publication Data

Morrill, Ann.
  Nonprofit organizations / Ann Morrill ; foreword by Ellen C. O'Connell.
    p. cm. — (Career launcher)
  Includes bibliographical references and index.
  ISBN-13: 978-0-8160-7958-2 (hbk. : alk. paper)
  ISBN-10: 0-8160-7958-7 (hbk. : alk. paper)
 1. Nonprofit organizations—Vocational guidance—Juvenile literature.
 2. Social service—Vocational guidance—Juvenile literature. I. Title.
  HD2769.15.M67 2009
  338.7'4—dc22

                                                    2009051273

Ferguson books are available at special discounts when purchased in bulk quantities for businesses, associations, institutions, or sales promotions. Please call our Special Sales Department in New York at (212) 967-8800 or (800) 322-8755.

You can find Ferguson on the World Wide Web at http://www.fergpubco.com

Produced by Print Matters, Inc.
Text design by A Good Thing, Inc.
Cover design by Takeshi Takahashi
Cover printed by Art Print Company, Taylor, PA
Book printed and bound by Maple Press, York, PA
Date printed: November 2010

Printed in the United States of America

10 9 8 7 6 5 4 3 2 1

This book is printed on acid-free paper.

Contents

Foreword

If you have picked up a copy of *Career Launcher: Nonprofit Organizations*, you have probably already started working in, or are contemplating a career in, what is often referred to as the "third sector." The third sector, defined in reference to the "profit" and "governmental" sectors, is also referred to as the civic, voluntary, nonprofit, or nongovernmental sector. As this book will reveal, the not-for-profit sector encompasses a broad array of jobs in fields as varied as health, education, humanitarian relief, homeless services, and medical research. Voluntary agencies employ people as social workers, executive directors, accountants, relief workers, administrators, and doctors. Engineers, water and sanitation specialists, receptionists, executive assistants, marketers, and finance controllers can also be employed in this sphere. Institutions such as hospitals, schools, assisted living centers, and homeless shelters are included under the broadly defined nonprofit heading. Agencies in this sector are also involved in advocacy for human rights and research for vaccinations and the cures for diseases such as cancer, ALS, hepatitis C, and HIV/AIDS. As you will read in this book, many of the jobs in the nonprofit sector have similar, if not identical, counterparts to positions in the private and government sectors. So what sets the nonprofit sector apart? Why launch a career in not-for-profit as opposed to the public or private sectors?

First, it is important to realize that given the breadth and scope of work incorporated under the heading of "not-for-profit," this sector encompasses a growing portion of the existing employment positions available in the United States today. Approximately one out of every 10 jobs in the United States is currently in the third sector. For that reason alone, you may be considering a career in nonprofit work. However, the common denominator for most people working in the nonprofit arena is most likely a social awareness that impels action. A career in this area can be extraordinarily rewarding. While many people may enter the field of nonprofit work out of a general sense of trying to "do good," or "give back," it is the challenges, intellectual and otherwise, and the force of mission and responsibility to humanity that compel most of us who stay in this area to make this work a lifelong career.

It is impossible to read the newspaper, listen to the radio, or watch television without being confronted with daily injustices, stories of death and disease, school failures, and gaps in the social fabric of society that leave individuals, families, and communities in need. The lack of adequate health care, inadequate educational systems, incurable diseases, homelessness, and illiteracy plague this country. Globally, you can find daily newspaper articles about human rights abuses, terrorism, brutal attacks on civilian populations, and the rape of women and children. If you travel, you may have been confronted with the atrocity of war and violence or have witnessed incomparable poverty or hunger. You may be personally affected by circumstances that make you uncomfortable being indifferent to the suffering of others. Or, you may simply want to give back, to help others enjoy freedoms, privileges, or the power of voice, opportunity, or education that you have known in your lifetime. You may be inspired by art or music and feel motivated to preserve a place in society for the arts. For many individuals, working in the nonprofit arena affords a chance to give voice to the silenced and oppressed. For others, the work is an inspiration, something that gives meaning to their lives beyond a job and a paycheck. For most, it is a challenge, a passion and a choice that enriches their lives and makes work an important facet of their entire being.

After over 25 years of work in the not-for-profit arena, knowledge and experience of the injustices, oppressions, and inequalities in the world have made it impossible for me to live in what the Dutch Protestant theologian Willem Visser't Hooft has called "a twilight between knowing and not knowing." I am simply compelled to act. As a vice president at the International Rescue Committee (IRC), an organization committed to helping victims of oppression and persecution around the world, I am confronted on a daily basis with the horrors of war, violence, and brutality. Since beginning work at the IRC over ten years ago, I have been to many of the world's most brutal corners, each one a heart of darkness where I have witnessed the consequences of some of the worst that man can do to man. The work that the IRC does domestically and internationally is life saving work. For over 10 years prior to my work at the IRC, I worked with homeless and disadvantaged youth in New York City. The support that the young men and women were given through the institutions that I worked with, and the positive impact that was made upon their lives and their futures, is undebatable.

In his acceptance speech for the Nobel Peace Prize in 1986, Elie Wiesel said, "We must always take sides. Neutrality helps the oppressor, never the victim. Silence encourages the tormentor, never the tormented. Sometimes we must interfere." I am no longer comfortable being indifferent, if I ever was. I am acutely aware of the serendipity of birth and the accident of fate. A desire to help or a commitment to a mission is an important start for work in the nonprofit sphere. It is what originally led me down this career path. But to be successful in this area of work, and to have an impact, one needs more than good-will or a vague desire to help. One needs to be professional.

My work in the nonprofit sphere continues to be rewarding and challenging, but it is not simply a desire to "do good" or to "give back" that prepares one for work in this area. Nonprofits are highly professional institutions that compete for human, financial, and other resources with the private and public sectors. They are accountable for the work that they do and to the beneficiaries of their work. My journey over the years in the nonprofit field has been punctuated by terrific mentors, lifelong friendships, and constant challenges and rewards. Many of the smartest people that I know work in the nonprofit sector. They are driven by the commitment to make a change and the challenge of the commitment. The issues with which many nonprofits grapple—war, disease, hunger, and disabilities—are some of the most complicated issues in the world. The people who are drawn to these causes are smart, educated, committed, and creative.

My nonprofit journey has compelled me to acquire advanced degrees in public administration and anthropology and to continue to obtain skills that help run effective and efficient organizations that have quantifiable and measurable impacts. As you start out on a career in the nonprofit sphere, do not underestimate the challenges, but rather embrace them. It is the challenges of nonprofit work as well as the missions of the institutions that make the work compelling and make the experience of working in this field extraordinary.

If you already have a sense of commitment to a cause, or a commitment to justice or equality; if you have a passion for the arts or an interest that drives you to the nonprofit sector, you have a terrific foundation for work in this field. The rest, however, entails professionalism, commitment, hard work, and creativity, much as you would find in the other two sectors of the economy.

Ellen C. O'Connell, MA, MPA
Vice President Administration and Board Relations
International Rescue Committee
New York, NY

Acknowledgments

During the summer of 2009 when I was writing the first draft of this book, I took a road trip with my ten-year-old son, Marcos, from Colorado to Indiana. On the way back home while driving through Kansas, I caught part of a Kansas City public radio program about homelessness in the large college town of Lawrence, Kansas. On the program, the former Lawrence mayor and several nonprofit social service agency directors were interviewed about how Lawrence was dealing with homeless issues, especially since the local Salvation Army had recently closed its doors.

As I listened I was struck by the compassion, cooperation, creativity, and skill of the nonprofit directors and representatives—their desire and ability to work together to get the homeless into decent local housing and to accommodate those who had been served by the Salvation Army. I was impressed with their resourcefulness and their sense of urgency in addressing the needs of the homeless community, as well as their knowledge and ability to communicate that knowledge in order to help educate their communities about who, exactly, makes up the homeless community. As I listened I realized how lucky I was to get to write this book about nonprofits because I got to interview incredible and dedicated individuals who were involved in helping others in so many different and interesting ways.

First and foremost I want to thank all the nonprofit professionals who were kind enough to answer my questions and to provide their experiences, expertise, and wisdom: Bill Shuey, Bruno Sukys, Lisa Marie Kramer, Sharon Dornberg-Lee, Ruth Ralph, Mohammed Muraee, Teresa Jacobsen, Elaine Peck, Nancy Lovett, Bernie Kosberg, Dwight Burlingame, Pamela Tims Bauduit, and Susan Wortman. What a group of truly inspiring human beings with, collectively, hundreds of years of experience in the nonprofit trenches. If I have done my job well, their words will motivate and educate all who borrow or purchase this unique guide.

I would also like to thank my friends and family for putting up with me over the last several months as I disappeared into books and my computer, as I Twittered to find out what nonprofits were Tweeting about, as I sent out pleas to everyone on Facebook that I knew was involved in nonprofit work (or knew someone who was), and as I explored thousands of nonprofit job and Web sites. Special gratitude goes to my husband Milton Ospina and sons Lucas and Marcos. Marcos, I know I will never be J. K. Rowling and you think my nonfiction stuff is boring, but I hope you will be proud of me nonetheless.

Finally, thanks to all of the people around the country and overseas who have chosen a career in the rich and diverse nonprofit world. Your work, as well as the tireless work of nonprofit boards and volunteers all over this country, has inspired me to want to work harder in my own community for meaningful change.

Introduction

You are likely reading a career book on nonprofits because first and foremost you believe in "doing good" as well as doing well. You understand that your role might be to make another's experience in the world a little healthier, a lot more informed, and possibly even a little more complicated, at first. You are not afraid of a challenge and you truly would like to make a difference—be it in a few people's lives or millions of people's lives.

Career Launcher: Nonprofit Organizations begins from the premise that you are just starting out in the nonprofit sector. It is a great book for you if you just completed college or graduate school and have your first nonprofit job; it also is a good read if you are looking to move from your current nonprofit position to another but are not sure how. Or perhaps you are a seasoned marketing executive tired of the corporate environment and interested in better understanding how your skills might translate to the nonprofit environment—this book is for you as well. This book will provide information that both deepens your understanding of the nonprofit sector as a whole and gives you a plan of attack—a launching pad—to help you to get the most out of your nonprofit job or future job.

Resources and Research

Books, newspaper articles, nonprofit job sites, philanthropy journals, and even blogs and social networking sites were sources for the writing of this book. There is a tremendous amount of information today about the nonprofit sector—written by consultants, blogged and Twittered about by those in the field, researched and presented by academic think tanks, and available on the thousands of nonprofit Web and social networking sites—that is accessible if you know how to look for it. There is also a dizzying array of nonprofit conferences, Webinars, and other forms of meetings that provide informational and networking opportunities for the nonprofit novice. All of these sources went into the researching and writing of this book, and the best ones are listed in Chapter 6 so that you can explore further on your own.

Interviews with a variety of people in the nonprofit field—from an academic with a long career teaching students about nonprofits, to executive directors with decades of experience, to a social worker who eventually became a foundation head, to a fund-raiser who wanted to work more directly with clients and decided to become a social worker—were also a crucial source of information for the writing of this book. These human resources provide perhaps that best insights and advice of all, and for that reason Chapters 1, 2, and 4 feature interviews with nonprofit professionals.

How to Use This Book

Career Launcher: Nonprofit Organizations can be read from the first to the last chapter, from the last to the first, or used as a handy reference for terminology and resources. While a complete front to back reading will give you the best overview of the nonprofit industry—including its history, current salary ranges, trends, job descriptions, strategies and tips for success, job terminology, and resources—you can also learn a great deal by exploring a single chapter that piques your interest or helps you to answer a pressing question.

To get a good sense of how this book is indeed a career launcher, scan the featured interviews and the many boxed features that are included throughout the book—boxes that give you fast facts about nonprofit issues and terminology, advice about keeping in touch, problem solving on the job, and technology and methodology that is on the cutting edge.

Here is a taste of what you will find in each chapter:

Industry History

Have you ever wondered why the nonprofit sector is considered a sector at all? After all, many of the jobs one finds in nonprofit work have counterparts in the for-profit and government sectors. In fact, the concept that nonprofits, especially charitable nonprofits, might benefit from seeing themselves as a group is a late development, not really taking form until the 1970s. As you explore the first chapter about the nonprofit industry's history in the United States, you will better understand some of the important *how* and *why* questions about nonprofits: how and why did the sector grow to be nearly one in every 10 jobs in the United States today? What events and trends helped shape voluntary action and philanthropy throughout U.S. history? What role did the government, federal legislation, private groups, and individual actors play? You might be in for some interesting surprises about some of these groups and individuals, such as the once "radical" beliefs of the early Masons and one of their U.S. leaders, Benjamin Franklin. To help you to understand this intriguing history, the chapter ends with an interview with the Center on Philanthropy's Dr. Dwight Burlingame, a leading expert in the field of the history of philanthropy.

State of the Industry

The second chapter discusses the state of the industry by providing statistics on wages and employment for key nonprofit fields and by delving into the some of the long- and short-term trends impacting the nonprofit sector today. Information from the Bureau of Labor Statistics, topical journals, newspapers, Web sites, and books by experts in the field help to create a comprehensive picture of the nonprofit sector. Peruse this chapter for statistics on the nonprofit jobs that earn the most and the least, the regions of the country that employ the largest number of people, the percentage of health care jobs that are in the nonprofit sector, and a thorough discussion of how economic downturns impact different parts of the industry. Finally, read the interview with social worker Sharon Dornberg-Lee about the tremendous opportunity in the senior/aging services nonprofit field and how and why this area has been successful even through difficult economic times.

In this chapter you might be in for some interesting surprises, including the following:

➡ Many associate nonprofits jobs with social service
   organizations, and yet jobs in this subsector only make
   up around 20 percent of all nonprofit employment.
➡ A number of well-known for-profit companies in
   recent years such as Patagonia and ConAgra have
   created nonprofits of their own.
➡ Almost half of the hospitals in the United States are
   nonprofit organizations.

On the Job

Chapter 3 provides an extensive list of jobs in several key subsectors of the industry. These descriptions will help you to understand who you should turn to within your organization with specific questions or issues, as well as paths for career advancement and links between positions or levels. Because the nonprofit sector includes so many jobs from so many sectors—from doctors and lawyers to job developers and janitors—special emphasis is placed on those jobs that are most common in nonprofit subsectors, as well as how those jobs function in unique ways within the nonprofit sector. For example, a for-profit and nonprofit agency may employ marketing professionals, but the focus, skills, job responsibilities, and relationships are often quite different.

Tips for Success

This chapter is a must-read for those who want to hear from the voices of nonprofit experience. You will get a thorough understanding of how to establish a professional reputation and do a first-rate job. Many career nonprofit employees provide insights into the ways they have been successful and offer advice that will help you to plan your career path in the industry. In other words, what does it take to make it and to enjoy what you do?

As you read through these tips and insights, you will likely notice many common themes: the importance of flexibility, listening, and good oral and written communication. While these themes reverberate throughout all sectors of the economy, this chapter provides a focused lens through which the nonprofit employee can better understand how they relate to various nonprofit jobs. It will help you to grapple with how you can be successful in the long run.

Finally, read the interview with executive director Bernie Kosberg, who provides insight into why the nonprofit Ramapo for Children—an organization he has directed for 24 years—has been successful for 85 years. What does Mr. Kosberg look for in an employee? How can you recognize a good board? How does he run a thriving program that works every day to carry out its mission? These questions and many more are answered in this chapter.

Talk Like a Pro

Do you ever wonder what the executive director is talking about when she gets into a conversation about *case statements* or the *PGI* (Philanthropic Giving Index) with the fund-raisers? What did she mean when she referred to *eleemosynary* organizations and what should you do when she calls on you and your colleagues to focus on *stewardship*? This chapter will answer these questions, providing definitions and explanations of key terminology and industry-specific jargon. It also includes terms that are used in many industries, but that are applied in the nonprofit sector in particular ways. For example, the concept of branding is common to many sectors, but nonprofit branding includes the need to focus on the nonprofit mission.

Resources

Would you like some book and Web site recommendations? Maybe you need to understand what kinds of training and educational programs could help you to further your career. This final chapter provides a selected list of resources for you to explore, including information on certificate and degree programs, useful blogs and Web sites, and books that focus on aspects of the industry such as fund-raising and its history. This is not an exhaustive list, but one with some of the best sources out there to help you to dig deeper into your chosen field.

Chapter 1

Industry History

As a nonprofit professional, an understanding of the history of your industry will reveal how historical events, legislation, and the work of past leaders and thinkers influence the industry today. Today, almost anyone can come up with an idea around a local or national need, and with a few other people, form an organization to raise awareness and money to fulfill that need. Most of us do not question or worry about our ability to freely associate with individuals and groups that share our interests and concerns. Yet this was not always the case. The story of early philanthropy is a fascinating one. Through the lens of its history, one can better understand the ongoing debates over the proper role of the government in private institutions, the power of wealthy individuals to shape policy, and how to take care of citizens in a capitalist and democratic society.

Early Volunteerism in Seventeenth-Century Colonial America

Much of early philanthropy has its roots in the English Statute of Charitable Uses of 1601, a parliamentary act with the purposes of assisting the poor, sick, and injured; providing funds for education; caring for orphans; providing tax relief; helping tradesmen; and constructing public buildings and other infrastructure. The statute makes clear that the assistance would come through the state and the church, and there was no question about this in anyone's mind.

The state granted gifts to local governments, the sanctioned church, and other public entities. In some of the British colonies in the United States this statute survived the American Revolution and was only overturned by legislative action in the nineteenth century.

In *Inventing the Nonprofit Sector*, the historian Peter Hall writes that in seventeenth-century America there were no private charitable agencies as we understand them today. While charters were being established in England at this time, early Puritans rejected the idea that the colonists themselves had the power to assemble or charter corporations without the approval and involvement of the government. For example, when Harvard College was formed in 1636 it was with the approval of the general court of the Massachusetts Bay Colony. While considered the first eleemosynary (nonprofit) corporation in the colonies, it was governed by Congregational ministers and government officials who needed the approval of the state. Its charter, curriculum, and professorial appointments were handled by the legislature for many years, even after the American Revolution.

In the colonial period, private schools and hospitals did not yet exist, as all institutions required state sanction. Moreover, volunteer activities in many New England towns were not voluntary in the true meaning of the word. Men were obliged to build roads and public buildings, and to fight in militias. If you did not "volunteer," you were fined. American "volunteerism" was in reality state-initiated donations of labor, money, and land for public purposes and uses. Townships and religious congregations were supported by taxes and enjoyed monopoly status.

The Changing World in the Eighteenth Century and the Growth of the Responsibility of the Individual

By the early eighteenth century, early American society and its values and traditions were beginning to change. The population was growing rapidly and while many early Americans still survived largely through subsistence farming, more farmers now sold their surplus, and artisans and farmers both relied on trade. Farmers who once worked only with family and relatives now needed to form larger groups to get their products to wider markets. As Americans became part of a market economy, they had new needs and were exposed to new ideas from England and Europe. England was experiencing great social, political, and economic changes, and political changes brought from England to Colonial America meant new ways of looking at the world and an individual's place within it. As Peter Hall eloquently explains in *Inventing the Nonprofit Sector*:

> The rise of voluntary organizations was rooted in powerful social, political, and economic forces, which, by the early eighteenth century, had begun to erode the authority of family, church, and government throughout the colonies. Shortages of land in older settlements, in encouraging geographical and occupational mobility, undermined the power of patriarchal families and the integrity of tightly knit communities. The reintegration of the colonist in the British commercial system challenged the established order: the crown's desire to enforce its commercial regulation forced the adoption of British legal forms in places where they had been resisted; the growth of markets encouraged individual entrepreneurship and the growth of commercial interests which advocated policies that worked against those of older elite, whose power was based on land, not money. In addition, the revival of trade also brought with it the radical political and economic ideas of the Enlightenment.

Enlightenment Comes to America

The eighteenth century brought the development of the idea of the "natural rights" of citizens—including the freedom of speech, the freedom to assemble, and the freedom to worship—and the rejection of oppressive governments. In *Documentary History of Philanthropy and Voluntarism in America*, Peter Hall writes that there was a progression of events during this time that are significant for the history of nonprofit organizations. In England some decades earlier, for example, these new ideas gave rise to mutual benefit organizations such as the Freemasons—a secret fraternal organization whose members assisted each other in hard times, provided entertainment venues, and shared resources and ideas.

Freemasons stressed individual worth and achievement and its members were tied to the rise of the Enlightenment—the idea that a community had both the ability and the obligation to work for self-improvement in order to perfect human society. Man's intellect, it was thought, could rescue the culture from despotism and tyranny. Although the Freemasons and subsequent fraternal groups were mostly concerned with mutual assistance and benefit, questions of broader charity, including civic improvement, became a central concern before long.

At the same time, religious thinkers and civilians were forming and espousing ideas that would encourage voluntary action. By the first decade of the eighteenth century in North America, Boston's Reverend Cotton Mather was disseminating writings that encouraged neighborhood societies to care for the needy in their communities, to form associations that would ensure that the sick and disadvantaged were helped, and to make certain that artisans and others could work collectively to help one another. Mather was also a tireless advocate for smallpox inoculation—which was very controversial at the time because it interfered with "God's providence." When he pushed for vaccination in Boston, riots erupted. He also advocated for the creation of libraries, temperance societies, and African American education. According to Hall's *Documentary History*, "For Mather...because the State and society were untrustworthy and subject to corruption, the source of a truly Christian community was, first of all, the reborn individual and, secondly, the capacity of such individuals to voluntarily associate for the purpose of bringing about the reformation and redemption of society and the State. This distinction between the two, together with an emphasis on voluntary associations as agents of change, was truly revolutionary."

Whereas Mather saw voluntary associations through a Christian prism, Benjamin Franklin reflected on Mather's ideas and translated them through his understanding of the Enlightenment. For Franklin, civic action should be carried out by secular associations, such as the Freemasons, of which he was an active member. In 1730, Franklin printed the first notice of Freemasonry in America in his newspaper, *The Pennsylvania Gazette*. A few years later, he held the title Provincial Grand Master of Pennsylvania. Other famous Freemasons and Franklin contemporaries included Paul Revere, Joseph Warren, and John Hancock.

Franklin went on to form other volunteer associations, including fire companies and a hospital in an effort to reform what he saw as an imperfect society. He was directly responsible for initiating the call for a hospital in Philadelphia in 1750 and urged more philanthropy in the following years to address the growing problem of the mentally ill. While it took a few decades to establish the first hospitals in Pennsylvania and Virginia, the process helped New Englanders to learn about forming boards, the responsibilities and succession of trustees, the establishment of bylaws, the development of meeting

Fast Facts

The Contributions of the Shriners

According to the Masonic Service Association Web site, during the late 1700s Freemasons were responsible for spreading the ideals of the Enlightenment. In the eighteenth and nineteenth centuries, Freemasons founded orphanages and homes for the elderly, helping to provide safety valves for some disadvantaged groups before a social structure existed in the United States. Today there are four million Masons around the world who contribute millions of dollars to children's hospitals and medical research.

Perhaps most significant are the Master Masons' contributions. Known as Shriners, these high-level masons are a charitable group that formed in New York after the Civil War to help fund social service projects. They were generally the wealthiest of the Masons whose dues helped support numerous philanthropic endeavors. Today many are familiar with Shriners because they participate in small-town parades riding in tiny cars and wearing odd outfits and hats. However, they also fund one of the country's largest nonprofit hospitals, the Shriner's Hospital for Children in Tampa, Florida. In total, the Shriners support 22 hospitals that provide specialty pediatric care, research, and teaching programs. Since 1922, Shriners Hospitals for Children have served more than 865,000 children.

styles, and decision-making by majority vote. While many uncertainties needed to be worked out, modern nonprofits echo early hospitals in important ways.

The Freedom to Assemble and the U.S. Constitution

After the American War of Independence (1775–83) and upon the creation of the U.S. Constitution, the freedom to assemble was legally protected. The Constitution made explicit the individual rights of expression, freedom of worship, and freedom to assemble. At the same time it also gave great power to the states, which meant that every state had its own laws governing corporations, associations, and charities.

However, the question of autonomy—the freedom to act without involvement from the state—for private voluntary organizations was far from solved. The freedom of the individual organization depended in part on its location—some states limited the growth and influence of private voluntary organizations. A court case involving Dartmouth College's ability to operate free of government interference had a big impact on the development of nonprofit organizations.

Dartmouth College Goes to the Supreme Court

Established in 1769 by royal charter, Dartmouth College was a small, successful Christian liberal arts college that the historian David Hammack describes as devoted to educating young men and Indians for the ministry. However, 45 years later the state of New Hampshire decided that, because Dartmouth accepted students from the public and was no longer under the English Crown's control, it was in fact under the state's control.

The state of New Hampshire insisted that Dartmouth needed a more practical focus—a focus on agriculture and engineering instead of on educating future ministers—and passed a law that compelled the Dartmouth board of trustees to include public officials to direct the new schools. In response, the Dartmouth trustees rejected the state's contention and went to court to preserve their right to control the college and its programs. In 1818, Dartmouth graduate and accomplished attorney Daniel Webster argued for the college and its trustees in front of the Supreme Court. Webster made a strong and emotional case for the trustees to operate free of the state's interference, and in 1819 the Supreme Court ruled in favor of Dartmouth. According to Hammack in *Making the Nonprofit Sector in the United States*, "The Dartmouth College Case established the legal rights of such private organizations and their trustees to manage their own affairs without constant and detailed interference by legislators."

The Increasingly Complex Society of the Nineteenth Century

By the early 1800s, volunteer associations gained momentum as Americans showed collective concern about issues like slavery, alcohol and drunkenness, and the poor treatment of the insane. Over time these associations grew to have national significance and many created national organizations with state and local chapters.

Churches began to organize around national denominations with educational and charitable programs, including national and international missionary efforts, and publishing arms. Fraternal groups such as the Freemasons and Oddfellows grew to hundreds of thousands of members. Added to this was the increase in the number of immigrants to the United States, who brought with them their own experiences with voluntary action. In 1835, French author Alexis de Tocqueville highlighted what he saw as the philanthropic spirit of Americans—which he considered one of the greatest strengths of United States—in his celebrated book *Democracy in America*.

During the Civil War (1861–65), private groups provided soldiers for the Union Army and volunteers to care for injured soldiers in the field. Many private groups also initiated effective fund-raisers to supply clothing and bandages to the wounded. After the war's end, there continued to be a need for these private groups to help rebuild the destroyed schools and communities and to educated newly freed slaves, who now were entitled to schooling. Fulfilling these needs was largely entrusted by the government to voluntary organizations. As the historian Arthur M. Schlesinger observed, the United States became "a nation of joiners" during second half of nineteenth century. This era saw a vast increase in business trade associations, trade unions, and advocacy groups promoting women's suffrage and prohibition. According to Hall, participation in associations was doubtless an extremely valuable education in democracy. Moreover, volunteer associations were created by women and African Americans, who could freely associate and advocate for specific causes even if they still could not vote.

The mid- to late nineteenth century was a time of other great transformations. The Industrial Revolution brought about huge changes in agriculture and transportation, as well as massive growth in urban factories. Between 1880 and 1900, U.S. cities grew by about 15 million people. The population growth of cities resulted from immigrants arriving from around the world. Additionally, a multitude of people flowed into cities from rural America between 1880 and 1890; up to 40 percent of rural townships shed significant portions of their populations due to migration. The U.S. government now had to deal with social welfare, health, transportation, and policing of growing cities. On the one hand, industrialization had meant rapid urbanization and the creation of jobs in factories; on the other, it meant that over time mechanized labor would replace human labor, leading to social unrest and an increase in poverty.

Early Philanthropy at the Dawn of the Twentieth Century

Around the turn of the twentieth century, industrialists like the "king of steel" Andrew Carnegie accumulated massive fortunes. While not what one could call a friend of organized labor while he owned Carnegie Steel, later in life he became a major benefactor in promoting philanthropy as a way of addressing the causes of poverty. "I resolved to stop accumulating and begin the infinitely more serious and difficult task of wise distribution," he said at the time. Carnegie believed that businessmen must use the skills that made

On the Cutting

Edge

The Russell Sage Foundation

The Russell Sage Foundation is still going strong today. It bills itself as "the principal American Foundation devoted exclusively to research in the social sciences...it is a research center, a funding source for studies by scholars at other academic and research institutions, and an active member of the nation's social science community." It was founded in 1907 by the widow of Russell Sage, Margaret Olivia Sage (1828–1918), a champion of women's rights, with an initial donation of 10 million dollars. Margaret then went on to direct its programs, including housing, public health, education, consumer credit, and industrial relations. According to the organization's Web site, "These programs led to legal reforms in building codes, workplace health and safety regulations, workmen's compensation and anti-usury laws."

A century later, the focus has shifted from a source of direct funding and information for private social agencies to a research association with the purpose of strengthening social science in order to illustrate and analyze the nation's ever-changing social problems. In recent years its programs have encouraged an interdisciplinary approach to understanding contemporary issues such as low skilled workers in today's labor market, the large recent wave of immigration, and the increase in economic inequality. In 2008 it listed its assets at over $250 million.

them rich to alter society for the better and that traditional charity was failing because it did not attempt to get at the roots of why people were poor.

Hall writes that Carnegie was influenced by the social Darwinism of the times, and that he and other wealthy industrialists expressed contempt for what they considered indiscriminately throwing money at the poor—money that encouraged sloth, alcohol abuse, and that often ended up in the hands of the "unworthy." Carnegie thought a more scientific approach that stressed the root cause of poverty would be most effective. To his credit, Carnegie put his money where his mouth was, donating tens of millions to establish parks, museums, libraries, and public halls such as Carnegie Hall in New York City. "Before Carnegie, most philanthropy had been small scale and conventional," writes Hall in *Inventing the Nonprofit Sector*. "After Carnegie, philanthropy, organized and focused through foundations, would assume an unprecedented scale and scope, becoming an important source of innovation in addressing problems of education, health, and social welfare." New laws in the early twentieth century also opened up the way for the wealthy to contribute vast sums of money. States enacted laws that allowed large-scale donations from groups and individuals like the Tilden Trust, Carnegie, and J. D. Rockefeller. Foundations established after the reforms include Rockefeller General Education Board (1901) to benefit black schools in the South, the Carnegie Endowment for the Advancement of Teaching (1905), and the Russell Sage Foundation (1907) to address social welfare issues on a national basis.

At the same time, the power of industrialists such as Carnegie and Rockefeller and their views of the failings of traditional charities were sometimes viewed warily. Many traditional charities and churches were suspicious of the power of the wealthy over social and political organizations and felt that their approach was inadequate. For instance, in focusing their incredible wealth on establishing libraries and universities to create permanent improvements in social conditions, and by being exceedingly concerned with the worthiness of the cause before giving money, some believed that these wealthy men and their institutions did not adequately address how rapid industrialization had contributed to the large-scale job loss at the turn of the century, which in turn created tremendous, immediate material needs for the newly impoverished.The famous social worker Jane Addams expressed the view, held by many churches as well, that charity was not just about economic provisions but it was about the forming of caring communities—the bonding of people together. Addams, who ran the now-famous Hull House, bristled against the new rules and regulations that were being imposed by Chicago's Bureau of Organized Charities, a group strongly influenced by the scientific philanthropists. However, she needed to work with them and thought that their approach could be humanized. The tension between those who believe that certain groups are more worthy of assistance and those who do not impose value judgments continues to play out in the United States today— at local city council meetings, on nonprofit boards, during government forums, and even in creating legislation such as the Welfare Reform Act of 1996. Not surprisingly, the concerns and approaches of social welfare pioneers such as Addams are still central to some nonprofits today, as are the ideological approaches of the early industrialists like Carnegie.

The First Community Trust

In 1910 a new kind of organization was formed in Cleveland by the Chamber of Commerce to address problems that charities were having, including a shrinking donor base, fraud, replication of efforts by many groups, and the ineffective use of resources. Requests for funds were growing, and in response the chamber formed an organization called the Community Chest. This group proposed an annual fund drive for all of the Cleveland charities, the result of which would then be divided among the most worthy charities. Cleveland banker Frederick Goff proposed creating a community foundation that would be able to receive charitable trusts and that would be under the authority of a board made up of bankers. Public officials and others formed a distribution committee that would determine which organizations would receive the funds.

The Community Chest broadened the donor base by asking for donations from Cleveland business employees. This successful approach spread very quickly and by the 1930s there were hundreds of towns and cities that employed the same idea. The Community Chest is considered the ancestor of today's United Way, one of the largest nonprofit organizations in the United States. By 2007, according to the 2007 *Nonprofit Times* study of America's largest nonprofits, the United Way had 1,300 local organizations and averaged close to four billion dollars in annual revenue.

The Professionalization of Volunteer Work

In the second and third decades of the twentieth century, voluntary associations that coalesced around causes continued to grow. Social groups like the Rotary, Kiwanis, and Lions clubs gained membership during this time, along with reform-oriented organizations that put pressure on public policies or laws that their members believed to be unjust. The NAACP (National Association for the Advancement of Colored People) formed to stop lynching and race riots; other associations formed to reform child labor laws and advance women's causes. During this time, individuals like Helen Keller were able to create programs for the blind, a group of people who had been educationally ignored and who were largely confined to institutions. Keller campaigned to better the living and working conditions of the blind and went on extensive fund-raising trips, often overseas, for the American Foundations for the Blind.

Along with the growth of these organizations came the professionalization of fund-raising, an area of nonprofit employment that is still vibrant and growing today. The early twentieth century witnessed the establishment and growth of fund-raising agencies that solicited funds for causes such as World War I and the establishment of universities. Foundations created by Rockefeller, Carnegie, and other wealthy philanthropists also began to rely on paid professionals.

The Expansion of the Central Government

During and after the Great Depression and World War II, the central government expanded its power in social and economic realms. This meant growth both in the for-profit and nonprofit sectors of the economy. For instance, the interstate highway system was built during the 1950s, and the government began to give subsidies to private industries such as the oil industry, which stimulated massive growth of the automobile industry. While government actions led to private-sector expansion, the government also encouraged the growth of charitable giving through tax breaks for donors, tax exemptions for charities, bigger grants and contracts for charities, and programs like the G.I. bill, which allowed an entire generation of returning soldiers to receive a higher education and led to an expansion of the university system.

Nonprofit Trends and Funding in the 1960s and 1970s

Beginning in the 1960s, a new ideological perspective saw the federal government as an important enforcer and protector of the rights of citizens. John F. Kennedy and Lyndon Johnston initiated what is known as the Great Society—a group of government programs that worked toward the elimination of poverty and racial injustice. During this period, the Civil Rights Acts of 1964 and 1967 were signed, Medicare and Medicaid were established (1965), and the women's movement for equality was thriving. Government institutions such as the National Institute of Health, the National Endowment for the Arts, and the National Science Foundation fueled the growth and transformation of nonprofits throughout the 1960s and 1970s.

Areas that before had been almost entirely for-profit—such as the performing arts and health care—were now the focus of numerous nonprofit groups. According to Hall (2003), by 1980 more than half of all human service nonprofit revenues came from the government. While government funding since the 1970s has gone up and down depending on the political climate and state of the economy—Ronald Reagan famously and successfully limited the reach and funding of the National Endowment for the Arts, for example—it continues to be a very important part of the revenue of many nonprofits organizations.

Increased public and private funding to nonprofits prompted an upsurge in other grassroots movements, such as civil rights and children's rights. The 1970s saw the growth of pro-choice and pro-life advocacy, as well as educational and environmental activism. More and more of these activities were run by professionals and policy experts, although many organizations continue to rely on volunteer bases to educate the public and to further their causes. Another trend during the 1970s was the decline in all-voluntary associations such as Kiwanis, sports leagues, and church-organized groups as a result of more isolated lifestyles. With the growth of suburbs and the ubiquity of the television, many Americans stayed home for their entertainment. After World War II, the United States also had an educated and mobile populace who wanted to be involved in narrowly focused organizations. Hall recounts a sharp decline after the 1960s in voting, attending public meetings, church attendance, participation in athletic associations like bowling leagues. In their place emerged the narrowly defined nonprofits that specialized in one kind of activity, advocacy, or service such as child care and health services.

In the 1970s and 1980s, nonprofits—many of whom were beneficiaries of the expansion of government programs—began to see

Everyone
Knows

501(c) (3)

A majority of nonprofits qualify as 501(c) (3) organizations, which mean they qualify for federal tax exemption under the Internal Revenue Code. Nonprofit groups that fall under 501 (c) (3) include charitable, religious, educational, scientific, and literary organizations, as well as those that test for public safety, foster national or international amateur sports competition, and prevent cruelty to children or animals. While nonprofit corporations can earn a profit, these profits are reinvested in the organization in order to further its cause. When an individual or group contributes to 501 (c) (3) groups, their contribution is tax deductible. Churches, schools, and other nonprofits with 501 (c) (3) status receive exemptions on property taxes, although the exemptions differ from state to state. Most groups that want to earn nonprofit status must submit state and federal applications. Churches, however, are automatically exempt and do not need to apply.

Additionally, groups that are classified as 501 (c) (3) are generally not allowed to work on political campaigns or advocate for a specific political candidate. Nonetheless, they can work on voter education activities (including presenting public forums and publishing voter education guides such as those the League of Women's Voters put out) and a percentage of their budget can be spent on lobbying. Nonprofits can also promote participation in the electoral process through activities like voter registration and get-out-the-vote drives as long as these campaigns are conducted in a non-partisan fashion.

Other tax-exempt organizations are classified as 501 (c) under the Internal Revenue Code, but their goals are not primarily charitable and donations to them are not tax-exempt. For example, chambers of commerce, real estate boards, boards of trade, and professional football leagues are not charitable organizations, they are 501 (c) (6) under the IRC, which means that they are not organized for profit.

themselves as a separate sector. This led to an increased desire to understand the role of the nonprofit—also referred to as the not-for-profit, third sector, independent sector, or voluntary sector—in society and to ensure that it played a viable role. To better understand the nonprofit sector, in 1973 prominent nonprofit leader John

INTERVIEW

The Nonprofit in Historical Perspective

Dr. Dwight Burlingame
Center of Philanthropy, Indiana University, Bloomington, Indiana

Could you describe some of the most important historical events or trends that have shaped nonprofit sector today?
I look to the colonial and pre-colonial period for the interest in helping others—not by commerce and not by government—which I'm defining as voluntary action intended for the public good, whether giving of time, or giving of money, or advocating for a social movement if the action is done voluntarily (not that it is not without pay, but that it is done voluntarily).

It is also important to point out that I am speaking of the early European-American development of philanthropy. After all, there were other civilizations here before, and they were practicing philanthropy in many parts of the country through activities like potlatch on the West Coast.

That concept of helping others is shaped fundamentally by the arguments that were taken in the Continental Congress in the creation of the Constitution, particularly in the First Amendment, and within the First Amendment the arguments for the freedom of assembly. The freedom to assemble, to do public good, guaranteed in the Constitution and in the First Amendment, is fundamental to why we have a nonprofit sector in America.

Out of the debate [in the Continental Congress about the freedom to assemble] comes the Federalist papers, especially Federalist #10, which is where [James Madison] looks at the establishment of all these different groups and how we could have tyranny: Should we be worried about this because we have all these little groups organizing and therefore they might overthrow the government that is being newly formed? But the argument put forth in Federalist #10 is that no, those [groups that might assemble] are very important because they will counterbalance each other and we will have the ideas developed and have the different approaches that will be a good thing for the new democracy.

In fact, [the arguments in Federalist #10] get played out over time through the legal system starting with the Dartmouth court case. And this [tension between the rights of independent groups to form and the power of the state to tell groups what to do] gets played out in the various states and different colonies. Some states argue for the independence and others don't, but ultimately the freedom to act individually in the public's good is accomplished by the end of 1840s—20 years [after Dartmouth]. And so we have the freedom of trustees to run nonprofit organizations and to determine what their mission will be, free of interference from the government.

Were there other forces at work that have helped form and shape the nonprofit sector today?
I think the governmental force, and secondly—in terms of the general history—religion was fundamental in shaping the nonprofit sector today, namely through freedom of religion to exist outside of the government, not to be interfered with by government, and to be exempt from government taxes. That belief in terms of how they would take care of others within the religious context is exemplified throughout our history.

Much of the nonprofit sector was created by religious organizations fighting for their own separate independence against other religious organizations that were trying to discriminate against them. These organizations created their own private religious schools and their own hospitals—social needs that in Europe in the early twentieth century were being provided by government. In the United States, this wasn't the case because of the religious debates among various denominations over who would be served.

The next big thing is capitalism and the creation of excess wealth. You really can't have philanthropy in the sense of redistribution of wealth through private action unless you have the creation of wealth. And capitalism did that. The redistribution of wealth from the Industrial Period, particularly the late nineteenth and early twentieth centuries led to the creation of many of America's major arts and cultural organizations, as well as higher educational institutions—the University of Chicago and Stanford come to mind.

If you had to identify any other reason why we have the nonprofit sector in America, in terms of large trends I would argue that those historical elements have now been integrated into what we would call our educational approach and how we think about public policy—our laws that have been enacted to allow for nonprofits and what their roles are in society. The expression of action independently—in elementary schools, in the households, in the universities—is now the culture. So the culture has been built up over time, and it's really the tradition that influences the continuation [of charitable work].

(continues on next page)

INTERVIEW

The Nonprofit in Historical Perspective (continued)

There is a common misconception that nonprofits are supported largely by private monies, but so much of the expansion of the sector has to do with the governmental involvement in nonprofits that began in the 60s and 70s. In your opinion, is this a good thing?

I believe that it is. The delivery of the service through private action—nonprofits—is a natural blend of how we are in the human condition anyway. Looking at the expectations and duties that we ascribe to government, and the efficiencies that we can get from voluntary action, and the inefficiencies of it, along with the efficiencies that government provides and what are its inefficiencies. If you think about it, what does government do best? They do two things best: One, they can redistribute wealth easily, through taxation. And two, the government has power—it can do it in a very efficient and just way. You eliminate free ridership, that's the important thing. In voluntary organizations, it's just not possible. If people choose not to give, they don't have to. A problem with philanthropy is in fact that it is voluntary and it suffers from amateurism in that sense.

When you think about those two things and the services that we need to provide in a civil society, the mixture of the two is natural—the blending of the sectors isn't problematic to me at all. The important point is the end result in how we are actually taking care of people—living with civility. People have dignity and respect, and I would argue that this mixture, this blending of government providing resources to nonprofits to provide service is really a strategic thing to do. You are accomplishing the social good, and you add the individual provision to the government provision— you engage them and actually generate more resources for that social good then if you just had government provision.

There are very few people in the American context that will give to government voluntarily. On the whole you don't pay more taxes than what you owe. Knowing that, how do you motivate these people to actualize their own interests? You provide opportunity to work and contribute to the causes one believes in and you create a more effective and dynamic nonprofit sector.

Are your students surprised by the role of government in nonprofits?

Yes, they are surprised about the size and scope, and they are pretty surprised about where the money comes from for the sector. When they originally come in they think that the nonprofits are funded by corporations and foundations and individuals, but in reality when they get into the coursework they find out that about 20 percent of the revenue of all nonprofits in United States (this of course excludes religion) comes from private sources—corporations, individuals, and foundations. Government funding is about 33 or 34 percent now. Fees for service are about 50 [percent]. The distribution of sources of revenue is often a shock to students.

What do you think about the trend in the recent past of the overlap between the for-profit and nonprofit sector. For example, what do you think about for-profit managers going into nonprofit work?

I think it has been a real mix. What people don't understand is the differentiation between business practices versus business motivation; it's where we get into trouble. It's perfectly great for the nonprofit organizations to use business practices when looking at issues of efficiency and effectiveness—those are important whether you are doing good or doing well. The adaption of business practices to voluntary action is a good thing. The problem is people come into management positions within the nonprofit organization out of business and forget to translate that service is the ultimate goal in the organization; it's not to make money. So when they look at the business practices—the balance sheets, spreadsheets, et cetera—they are interpreting it in the context of the business environment rather than the nonprofit environment—I think that's the problem. So we have to do a better job in terms of education, which is what we try to do all the time here. It's mentioned a lot in our courses. In our nonprofit economics course, for example, understanding the difference in nonprofit economics and for-profit economics and then its application to practice is an important part of the course.

Do you find that students who come in to the graduate courses of nonprofit management have a better understanding of for-profit models?

In our students there is a definite difference in the master's students coming straight out of college versus the people who have been out in the field coming back. Students coming directly from undergraduate

(continues on next page)

INTERVIEW

The Nonprofit in Historical Perspective (continued)

work know they want to study and then work in a field that will improve society. The older generation coming back or transferring out of business and coming in are a bit more seasoned and savvy, and they don't always quite have the idealism to the same degree. But they have been in the business sector and they are looking for a change to have a greater impact by working for the social good.

As a professor of the history of philanthropy, what kinds of responses do you get from students to your courses?
Our M.A. degree is unique because of its focus on the history of social and ethical foundations of the nonprofit sector—understanding the *why* question instead of the *how to do it* question. Most students also take electives in the *how to do it* part, as they think about preparation for graduation and how to best prepare for work in the marketplace... There is around a 95 percent satisfaction rate with our approach— having it based on *why* we do it, the understanding from the liberal arts perspective.

D. Rockefeller initiated a Commission on Private Philanthropy and Public Needs (called the Filer Commission after its chairman John Filer), bringing together the best and brightest leaders in the field. Out of this commission came a two-year study dealing with nonprofits as employers; as providers of health, educational, and cultural services; and as political forces that could help to shape policy. A few years later, Yale University's Program on Nonprofit Organizations was formed to educate upcoming nonprofit leaders and to conduct much-needed research.

Nonprofits as Major Employers

"We have to keep in mind that the nonprofit sector is now one out of every ten in the employment force and so when you tally up the various fields and numbers, it's very significant," Dr. Dwight Burlingame

After completing the master's in your program, what kinds of jobs do your students find? Have you tracked where they go? What are the main areas they go into?

Well, 10 percent go into foundations and granting organizations of some sort, probably 40-50 percent go into fund-raising positions, and the remaining 50 percent or so go into various jobs within the sector: they are in program management or program development in a nonprofit, or they become the executive director of a small nonprofit.

When the economy turns down, do you have any words of encouragement for those starting out in the nonprofit field?

Yes, if you are in a nonprofit, this is the perfect opportunity to be doing the stewardship with your current donors and developing that rather than asking them for money, to the same degree at least. You still have to do the fund-raising; you still have to ask for money and you need to focus on really shoring up and cleaning up your potential donor lists. This is really the time for stewardship—educating and communicating to the donors about how their dollars are being used and will be used.

That's number one. Secondly, it's an opportunity to really do a very thorough assessment of your program, which can identify where you are now, something you may not want to be continuing to do, and where you can organizationally change to get the person in the right seat on the bus.

tells Career Launcher. The sheer number of new nonprofits in the United States between 1940 and 2005 demonstrates the tremendous importance of both societal changes and government expansion and action. In the 1940s, there were 12,500 charitable tax exempt organizations, 180,000 religious congregations (that did not need to apply for tax exempt status), and around 60,000 non-charitable nonprofit organizations such as unions and fraternal associations. In 2005, there were 600,000 charities, 400,000 religious congregations, and 600,000 non-charitable nonprofits.

Remarkably, a million and a half groups, congregations, and organizations exist today to serve communities around the United States. These organizations are funded by the government and by private grants, fees for services, individual donors, and foundations. Some rely primarily on volunteers and volunteer boards of directors to further their goals, but many employ paid professionals from a multitude of fields and backgrounds. In many ways, these organizations are run like businesses.

According to the Foundation Center, by the early 2000s nonprofits employed 9.5 percent of the population of the United States. In other words, 12.5 million people around the country work in the nonprofit sector today. Forty percent of industry employees worked in health services, 22 percent in education and research, 18 percent in social and legal services, 12 percent in religious organizations, and 4 percent in civic, social, and fraternal organizations.

What Drives the Nonprofit Industry?

Over the centuries, societal needs in the United States were often easy to see and understand, especially before the social safety nets such as Medicare were in place. For example, those that did not or could not fight in the Civil War saw that the soldiers needed bandages and medicine and found a way to provide the basics to as many as they could. Helen Keller was blind and deaf and knew that if conditions were to change for others like her, she would have speak out and to act to find the funds to do it.

Both Broad and Narrow Issues Drive Nonprofit Actions

Today, societal needs are often more narrowly focused and not as widely agreed upon. Whereas cancer research is a need that is almost universally acknowledged—and is funded by individuals as well as private and public funds—immigrant services such as job training or financial help often have a narrower financial and volunteer base from which to draw. The political and economic climate of the times impacts the opportunities in the nonprofit sector.

Another nonprofit field that has changed and expanded has to do with the environment, which is more widely believed to be in peril today than ever before. There has been a tremendous change in perception and understanding of environmental issues since George H.W. Bush dubbed Al Gore "Ozone Man" in 1992. Today, there is greater funding for "green" nonprofits, a number of which are international in scope and working on environmental concerns both abroad and in the United States.

The Impact of the Economy

Clearly, the driving forces behind a nonprofit's success cannot be divorced from the economic climate. As one executive director, William Shuey, wryly put it, a nonprofit is market-driven: "You can't beg if no one has money to dole out." When foundations lose half of their money in a year, when individuals like Bernard Madoff abscond with the wealth of potential major donors and entire charities, and when extensive job loss impacts a family, a company, or an entire country's bottom line, the nonprofit engine will slow down even while needs increase. In late 2008, for example, the *New York Times* reporter Stephanie Strom wrote that "The Carl and Ruth Shapiro Family Foundation, which supports organizations like the Brigham and Women's Hospital in Boston and the Jewish Federation of Palm Beach in Florida, said it lost $145 million, or 45 percent of its assets at the end of last year, because of investments with Mr. Madoff."

The Role of Effective Organizing

In changing times, the importance of effective organizing becomes amplified—both when the organization is very young and the boards are being developed, and when it is operating in a drastically changed social, economic, or political climate. Organizing requires superb marketing skills to sell the nonprofit's product—be it voter registration or affordable housing—which involves innovative development and use of human and capital resources. Organizing means not just telling the public about the organization's mission, but getting them informed and excited to be on board—as donors, volunteers, and as clients.

Further, the willingness to form connections and partnerships with other groups and the readiness to see weaknesses in the existing organization help drive a nonprofit's success. Many nonprofits are taking a hard look at maintaining an involved donor base and avoiding the duplication of efforts with other groups and the ineffective use of resources. In many areas, small nonprofits that have the same mission can save significant overhead costs by forming coalitions. According to *Crain's Detroit Business* reporter Sherri Begin, funding sources expect nonprofits to look closely at their business models and will reward those that show measurable, quantitative success. The organizations that will be at the forefront of the changing nonprofit sector are those that address these concerns with precision and creativity.

A Brief Chronology

1601: The English Statute of Charitable Uses is written.

1636: Establishment of Harvard College in Boston, MA.

1700s: Enlightenment/Age of Reason moves across America.

1710: Cotton Mather writes *Bonifacius*.

1730: Freemasons establish first group in America.

1770s: First hospitals formed in Pennsylvania and Virginia.

1775–83: American War of Independence.

1787: The Federalist #10 is published, which asks whether it is better to control a faction through removing it or through controlling its effects. James Madison argues for the latter and in fact the freedom to assemble in the Constitution's First Amendment is the direct result of that argument winning out; U.S. Constitution—the world's longest surviving written charter of government— is adopted.

1791: Ratification of First Amendment to the Constitution; the ten amendments are known as the Bill of Rights.

1819: Resolution of the Dartmouth Case.

1861–65: Civil War further encourages establishment of voluntary groups to aid in the war effort, including the founding of the International Committee of the Red Cross in 1864, one of the precursors to modern international nonprofits.

1880–1900: Industrial Revolution takes place throughout America.

1900–10: Establishment of first major foundations, including Carnegie and Rockefeller.

1910: First Community Chest established in Cleveland.

1913: Congress exempts charities from paying federal income tax.

1917: The Revenue Act of 1917 allows taxpayers to deduct charitable contributions from their federal income tax.

1935: Charitable deductions are extended to corporations.

1940s: Massive expansion of U.S. central government.

1942: Federal withholding of income tax.

1973: Filer Commission, or the Commission on Private Philanthropy and Public Needs, conducts a comprehensive, multidisciplinary survey of the nation's nonprofit sector and concludes that the nonprofit sector faced serious problems, including a shortage of pertinent research and no academic programs to prepare nonprofit leaders.

1976: Filer Commission leads to the creation of nonprofit programs, such as Yale University's Program on Nonprofit Organizations, the first research center of its kind.

1980: The Independent Sector is formed as a permanent consortium dedicated to strengthening nonprofit organizations through research, education, and advocacy.

Chapter 2

State of the Industry

A quick search on the *Nonprofit Times* Job Search board yielded an interesting snapshot of the incredible breadth of the nonprofit sector in 2009: The Silver Bay YMCA of the Adirondacks needed a CEO and would pay between $100,000 and $130,000 for the right person. The environmental nonprofit Audubon needed an assistant comptroller with at least seven years of experience in nonprofit and public accounting. The Association for Insured Retirement Solutions needed a writer and Web content designer for the organization's Web site and would pay between $45,000 and $60,000 a year. The lists go on, including job descriptions for direct marketers, interns, fund-raisers, and bilingual office assistants.

In a sector so large and diverse, how does the new employee make sense of what, exactly, might be out there today and in the future? What kinds of fields make up the nonprofit industry? Moreover, how is this sector as a whole doing? To answer these pressing questions about the state of the nonprofit sector requires a broader understanding of the professions involved as well as how these professions relate to other sectors in the economy.

What Is a Nonprofit?

In 2009, there were a million and a half nonprofit organizations operating in the United States. Their budgets range from almost nothing for all-volunteer organizations to millions of dollars. The common denominator for those working in this sector is that the organizations for which they work have a benefit to the public that the community at large does not provide either because it chooses not to or because it cannot. Another commonality among nonprofits is that their nonprofit organizations are mission-driven, rather than profit-driven. Although this sector includes organizations that do indeed make a profit through services or goods that are sold, these profits must be reinvested in the organization itself.

In some cases the nonprofit organization serves as a complement to the work of public institutions that are supported by tax revenues. According to Lester Salamon and S. Wojciech Sokolowski in a 2005 Bureau of Labor Statistics (BLS) report, "Included within [the non-profit] sector are more than half of the Nation's general hospitals; nearly half of its higher education institutions; most of its family service agencies; almost all of its symphonies; substantial proportions of its nursing homes; and most of its homeless shelters, soup kitchens, community development agencies, and hospices—to name just a few."

Major Centers for Nonprofits in the United States

While nonprofits can be found all around the United States, in cities as large as New York and towns as small as Greencastle, Indiana, the national headquarters of the largest nonprofits are typically in big cities, and many of these are on the East Coast. Nonprofits have good reason to be in major urban centers and near Washington D.C. as they often rely on Eastern foundations and wealthy donors for grants and donations. Moreover, some have goals related to impacting federal legislation. Being within earshot of the political movers and shakers requires being close to state capitals or Washington D.C. Under lobby laws established over 30 years ago, 501(c) (3) nonprofits can spend up to a defined percentage of their budget for lobbying without threatening their tax-exempt status.

According to the *Nonprofit Times*, the 10 largest nonprofits in 2007 (those that created the most income in one fiscal year) were:

1. American Red Cross (Washington, D.C.)
2. YMCA of the USA (Chicago)
3. United Jewish Communities (New York)
4. Catholic Charities USA (Alexandria, Virginia)

5. The Salvation Army (Alexandria, Virginia)
6. Goodwill Industries International (Rockville, Maryland)
7. Memorial Sloan-Kettering Cancer Center (New York)
8. Boys & Girls Clubs of America (Atlanta, Georgia)
9. Habitat for Humanity International (Americas, Georgia)
10. Boy Scouts of America (Irving, Texas)

Of these ten, the national headquarters for eight are located in the East, one in the Midwest and one in the Southwest. All of these nonprofits with the exception the Memorial Sloan-Kettering Cancer Center have state and/or regional offices around the country to help serve their constituencies. Some also have international offices that provide yet more opportunities for employment. Together, these top ten organizations employ tens of thousands of people around the country in professions as diverse as financial consultants, computer technicians, project coordinators, doctors, writers, social workers, nurses, lawyers, chief financial officers, retail store managers, cashiers, customer service representatives, and fund-raisers. Just about any career found in the for-profit sector exists in nonprofits, and the range of salaries can be almost as broad.

Recent studies have provided good data on where the most people are employed in the nonprofit sector. According to the 2005 BLS report, "Nonprofit employment is particularly dense in the northeastern part of the country, reaching 13 percent of all private employment in the New England States and 12.2 percent in the mid-Atlantic region . . . By contrast, nonprofit employment accounts for 5.4 percent of total private employment in the West South Central region, 6.2 percent in the Pacific region, and 6.3 percent in both the East South Central region and the Mountain region."

For-Profit versus Nonprofit Industries

In 2007, the BLS conducted a wage comparison of nonprofits with for-profit private industry and government employers. Some of their most intriguing findings include that, taken as whole, full time workers had higher hourly wages in nonprofits than in private industry overall, but nonprofit managers earned less on average than for-profit managers. Office and administrative support employees had wages very similar to their for-profit counterparts. The 2005 BLS report had slightly different findings, reporting that "nonprofit wages, although generally lower than those of for-profit enterprises or government, actually equal or exceed for-profit wage rates in the industries in which both sectors are involved."

Managers of nonprofits come into the field with many motivations, and not all of them are financial. Amy Butler of the BLS, citing important studies on wage compensation and differentials, provides the following synopsis and analysis in a 2009 BLS report, "Wages in the Nonprofit Sector: Occupations Typically Found in Educational and Research Institutions":

> According to the labor donation hypothesis, workers in the nonprofit sector are willing to donate a portion of their paid labor and receive lower wages because they obtain satisfaction from the fact that their efforts achieve altruistic goals. Also, nonprofits might pay lower wages and compensate their workers with employer-provided benefits or other favorable job characteristics such as a flexible work schedule. On the other hand, some nonprofits might actually pay *higher* wages because nonprofits do not benefit from the cost reductions of paying lower wages in the same way that for-profit employers do. In addition, nonprofits may choose to hire better quality workers in order to produce a better quality product or service and pay these employees higher wages.

Employment and Wages in the Nonprofit Sector Today: Social Services

Journals and online publications that address the nonprofit industry often have as their main focus the lifeline organizations—the social service (also called human service) nonprofits that serve at-risk populations by providing food, shelter, basic health care, job development, and other social services that would otherwise not be provided or that complement what the government provides. Overall data from 2005 indicate that human service jobs make up close to 20 percent of all nonprofit employment and include areas such as family services, child day care, and job training. Jobs at service organizations include but are not limited to CEOs (known in some organizations as the president or the executive director), fund-raising and development directors, director of volunteers, social workers, health care workers, caseworkers, job counselors, child care workers, and administrative staff.

Wages for people in this sector vary widely from job to job, region to region, and profession to profession. According a 2009 BLS survey, social service workers (including social workers, counselors, and religious workers) earn an average of $17.68 at private nonprofits. Breaking it down even further, the 2009 survey reports: "Social workers, a group that includes specific occupations such as family, public health, and mental health social workers, earned $19.49 per hour at nonprofits, less than their counterparts at local governments ($25.96 per hour)."

According to a 2001 article on trends in the social service nonprofit sector, Kirsten A. Grønbjerg provides the following useful analysis by comparing social/human services to other parts of the sector:

> The human service field is also distinct by its relatively low levels of institutionalization, especially when compared to health and higher education. Except for the growing importance of the Medicaid program, there are no dominant national funding sources. Nor are there well-developed and powerful professional groups or highly developed markets or communication structures. As a result, there is considerable variation within the organization field.

Employment and Wages: Health Care

The nonprofit sector includes fields not identified exclusively as nonprofit because they are also part of the for-profit sector, such as health care. The world renowned Mayo Clinic is a nonprofit hospital, yet some doctors working there make as much as or more than doctors in for-profit hospitals. In fact, a 2005 BLS study by Karen P. Shahpoori and James Smith found that "the average hourly rate for all workers in private for-profit hospitals was lower than the average hourly rate for all workers in private nonprofit hospitals" and that salaries for doctors and nurses in the for-profit and nonprofit sectors were nearly identical.

Health care is an important focus because according to the BLS, organizations that provide health services make up 37 percent of the revenues of the entire nonprofit sector. More than half of all hospitals in the United States and around 30 percent of nursing homes are nonprofits. According to the most recent BLS surveys, doctors at nonprofits averaged more per hour at $55 per hour, significantly higher than doctors who worked for state or local government institutions, where they average just over $40 per hour. Registered nurses (RNs) earn almost the same average hourly salary whether they work for nonprofits, for-profits, or the government, averaging $30 an hour. Clinical technicians and vocational nurses earned nearly the same amount (between $16 and $18 per hour) whether they worked for nonprofits, state or local government, or private for-profit organizations.

Health care management is considered a separate field, but many in this field work for nonprofit hospitals and health facilities, making them nonprofit workers as well. The BLS *Occupational Handbook for 2008–09* sees this area as a growing one, and the employment of medical and health services managers is expected to grow 16 percent between 2006 and 2016. The BLS reports that the health care industry is expected to continue to expand, and therefore so will the managerial jobs that help the business of health care run smoothly—be it in a low-income clinic setting or a health care facility catering to seniors.

Employment and Wages: Education

On the education front, private universities such as Harvard and Stanford are nonprofits, as are many private secondary and elementary schools around the nation. Teachers are likely to work for the nonprofit sector, as close to half of all educational institutions are nonprofits. According to a 2005 BLS report, 15 percent of all nonprofit workers are in the education field. In fact, very few private colleges and universities are for-profit establishments. A nonprofit survey by the Independent Sector Nonprofit Almanac in 2001 revealed that the health and education services combined employed 64 percent of all workers in the nonprofit sector.

Teachers who work in first grade through high school classrooms are largely employed in public (government funded) schools and over half are represented by unions. Preschool teachers and other private school teachers, whether for-profit or nonprofit, do not usually have union representation, and that can mean lower salaries. Butler's 2009 BLS report shows that the average earnings of all workers categorized as part of education, training, and library occupations in nonprofit establishments were $29.33 per hour for 2007. Elementary and middle school teachers in nonprofits earned, on average, $25 per hour, and secondary teachers at nonprofits earned an average of $34 per hour (almost the same as public school teachers). Interestingly, postsecondary teachers earned slightly more at nonprofits, $48.82 per hour, than at public or private for-profit schools.

Obviously, these statistics are averages for a very large country with diverse needs. Teachers in science, math, and bilingual education are predicted to be in high demand and have strong employment opportunities through 2016; rural and inner-city schools will also provide more teaching jobs than suburban areas. Geographical areas like the West and the South, especially Nevada, Arizona, and Georgia, are growing quickly and will need many new teachers. Others changes, such as increased funding in some areas for all-day preschools and an increase in preschool population over the next decade, will mean a growth in child care and preschool-center needs, many of which are nonprofit organizations.

The *Nonprofit Times* Survey: Nonprofit Management

It is nearly impossible to address current wage and employment statistics for all nonprofit jobs because the BLS breaks down most of their statistics by occupation, not sectors of the economy. However, there are some studies that focus on jobs typically found in nonprofit management, and which cross many areas of nonprofit jobs, especially health care, education, and social service fields. A useful place to start to understand the current state of the nonprofit industry, especially for those in executive and management positions, is the yearly *Nonprofit Times* surveys on wages and employment.

The most recent *Nonprofit Times* survey demonstrates that salaries tend to fluctuate depending on geographic region. The mid-Atlantic, West, and New England regions had the highest paid executive directors and the West had the highest paid development directors. Overall, coastal area salaries were higher than salaries in the Midwest and the South, although salaries in Florida tended to be high in 2007 because nonprofits there had difficulty filling positions, and the cost of living in major urban areas—where most nonprofits were located—was high. In the Northwest, where salaries have traditionally lagged behind other areas, salaries appear to be catching up.

Not surprisingly, the best-paid CEOs worked for organizations whose annual budgets were greater than $50 million. Men were twice as likely to be CEOs of organizations that generated $50-million-plus in revenue and women were twice as likely to lead organizations with revenue under $500,000. The average salary for a female CEO in 2008 was just over $103,000 compared to just over $130,000 for the average male CEO. The study also revealed which jobs are currently doing the best in terms of salary increases. For example, fund-raising is an area of strength today in the nonprofit sector, whether working at a nonprofit hospital or college or a multi-service organization. The major gifts officer and the development director had the greatest salary increases overall from 2007 to 2008, at just over 6 percent and 5 percent, respectively. Executives in other positions such as program director, webmaster, and chief financial officer, received very small increases in salary for that year, which did not keep up with inflation. Two salaried positions, the director of volunteers and the director of human resources, experienced a slight salary decrease from 2007 to 2008. The national average salary for the executive director/CEO/president increased from approximately $117,000 in 2007 to $119,500 in 2008.

Current Trends in the Industry

Have you ever wondered how your job or potential job fits into the whole of the nonprofit sector and what the future holds for you? A look at current trends that impact nonprofit structures, employment, opportunities, and missions might help answer these questions. Some of these trends might be industry-wide, affecting a wide swath of the nonprofit sector, while others might be specific to just a few fields, such as health care. Further, it is valuable to understand what the experts in the nonprofit field—be they researchers or leaders of large and small nonprofits around the country— are writing and saying about current and future trends in the industry.

Fee for Service a Growing Nonprofit Trend

For the past several decades, federal and state governments have been central to the funding of many nonprofit organizations. Nonprofits can directly receive grants or receive federal grant money through the state or city in which they operate. According to a recent report by the nonprofit OMB (Office of Management and Budget) Watch, federal monies may also be paid out to nonprofits as a fee for services, such as when nonprofit health organizations are reimbursed by the federal health insurance program for meeting health needs in a particular community (for example, for Medicaid). In 2006, federal funds provided $135 billion to nonprofits under the Medicare program and then another $10 billion in other kinds of fee for service payments.

Fast Facts

Signs of the *Nonprofit Times*

There are key movers and shakers in the nonprofit field that are challenging the way nonprofits think about themselves, restructuring the way they do business, and providing fresh and innovative ideas that have led to real societal change. Melinda Gates of the Bill and Melinda Gates Foundation and Wendy Kopp of Teach for America are two of the better known nonprofit leaders, yet there are numerous others whose work and words can inspire nonprofit professionals and help them to strategize and work within their own organizations. A great place to bone up on the year's best and brightest in the nonprofit industry—including the leaders of philanthropies, researchers, and executive directors of a wide array of nonprofits around the United States—is the *Nonprofit Times* "Power and Influence Top 50" guide. The *Nonprofit Times* admits that this list is not in any way scientific, but for someone new to the industry it is a good starting point if you want to do further research on what it takes to make it to the top of the nonprofit world.

Nonprofit hospitals and colleges have historically charged a fee for service—for tuition, from an individual's insurance company, and so forth—but so do some human service organizations. To charge a fee and not be taxed by the government, however, the service must be directly related to the nonprofit's mission and as a general rule the organization must charge less than a for-profit organization would charge. In the case of nonprofit educational institutions, the schools must show that they provide substantial needs-based scholarships in order for them to obtain or maintain their nonprofit status. Health clinics that cater to low-income communities often charge their clients fees on a sliding scale determined by a family's or individual's needs. Some child care agencies charge fees in much the same way. Even conservation organizations can charge a fee when they provide consultants and technical expertise, such as guidance on identifying and protecting lands for potential public use. The difference between for-profits and nonprofits is that the fees must be reinvested in the nonprofit and are not to be redistributed (for example, to shareholders).

Challenges to Nonprofit Status

The nonprofit status of organizations is being challenged more and more as nonprofits begin to look like businesses. Congress and local tax assessors are starting to ask questions about whether a nonprofit hospital or university is giving enough charity or financial aid to earn its property tax exempt status. According to a *New York Times* article, "Tax Exemptions of Charities Face New Challenges," by Stephanie Strom, one reason for this is that state and local governments are feeling the pressure of dwindling coffers because of lower tax revenues. Local governments can lose billions of dollars on unrealized property taxes from nonprofits.

Should a day care center be tax exempt if it charges all families the same price per child? When universities and hospitals have large reserves of accumulated wealth, should they still be considered charities? How are they different from for-profits that must pay taxes? These are some of the questions being raised by elected officials.

According to Strom, some nonprofit leaders are responding with salient concerns of their own: The government, they claim, wants nonprofits to run themselves more like a business with an eye to the bottom line; but if they do, the state wants to tax them like a business, even though they serve at-risk communities that for-profits do not or cannot serve as cost-effectively. Strom interviews Jon Nelson, director of the nonprofit RSI, Inc., in Duluth, Minnesota, who says this is a losing proposition. RSI, Inc., has served the mentally disabled for 30 years, since the state began shutting down its homes for the disabled. He warns that neither for-profits nor the state are willing to take on these clients, and that his nonprofit provides services at a much lower cost. But if RSI, Inc., were to lose its tax exempt status, it would be forced to pay close to $110,000 in property taxes, causing substantial cuts in programs and services.

Nonprofits and Pressure to Act Like For-Profits

Over the last few decades, nonprofits have been increasingly encouraged to act like for-profits with respect to measuring success: If they can quantify their results for donors, the government, and foundation funders, these entities can best determine which organizations are most worthy of their support. The emphasis is on accountability: the funding entity will continue funding when and if the nonprofit shows it deserves the money.

While measuring success can be useful, it is tricky. A health clinic can quantify the number of immunizations it has provided to children without health insurance, shots that by themselves provide a concrete result: protection against the chicken pox or TB, for instance. If a foundation or government organization has provided these funds to several agencies, the funders can look at the results and determine the clinics that have made most efficient use of their funds. But how does a literacy nonprofit quantify the impact of reading to a preschool child without access to books at home? The nonprofit can measure the volunteer hours logged, the number of free books it hands out, and the kinds of interactions with the children and their parents, but to quantify the impact an hour a week might have in terms of furthering the child's literacy is difficult. Not all results are easily measured.

Moreover, corporate and banking industry tribulations have made the entire country a little uncertain of the efficacy of some business management practices. If it is accountability that is important, many in the public and nonprofit sector say the for-profit world should also walk the talk. That said, nonprofits over time have adopted some for-profit business practices in order to improve their products or services and to promote financial discipline.

To become more business-like, nonprofit boards often recruit people from the for-profit sector for their business acumen and their money and influence. For the same reasons, nonprofits may hire executive managers from the for-profit world. In some cases, CEOs come in and create profitable entities within the nonprofit organizations. When this happens at a nonprofit, the staff—especially those that work directly with clients—sometimes fear that the board and senior management will be more focused on the bottom line and not on the nonprofit mission. This diversification might be scary to some who fear that the nonprofit will shift focus, but in hard economic times when private grant, state, and federal dollars are slow in coming, expanding into a revenue-generating area can help diversify the funding sources and even potentially save nonprofit jobs and charitable services.

Business leaders joining the nonprofit sector or business consultants who want to venture into nonprofit consulting have much to learn from nonprofit managers and researchers. Nonprofits tend to be much more complex than for-profits of the same size: a nonprofit CEO must direct diverse stakeholders and populations, including managers, a board of experts, community representatives, clients and their representatives, volunteers, members (if there is a membership element), and those who provide services. Additionally, they must manage relationships with government grantors, contributing businesses, and individual donors. The intricacies of the nonprofit funding structure leads to what Bill Landsberg, an attorney and the executive director of The Pikes Peak Foundation for Mental Health, calls multiple bottom lines.

Moreover, according to Landsberg, some recent business-related trends have mixed results: Outside consultants are brought in and asked to assess the finances and risk management, sometimes for-profit models for management are introduced, stressing productivity and budgets over the mission. Writes Landsberg in the *International Journal of Not-for-Profit Law*, "Even the lexicon of business has effloresced in the nonprofit world." He goes on to argue that when charities look less and less like charities, donors are sometimes less likely to give to them.

For-profit models can create tensions between management and staff. Landsberg calls these tensions the result of "psychological distancing" and emphasizes that different kinds of people are drawn to the different positions within an organization. "Management's focus on financial health and program staff's concerns with mission delivery create two camps in the organization . . . each failing to understand and communicate with the other." Landsberg emphasizes that he is not devaluing the important role of for-profits and their expertise, but rather stressing that they are different entities and that the viability of a nonprofit depends on the CEO's understanding this difference.

Increase in Nonprofit Management Programs

Since the 1970s and 1980s, academic programs to prepare nonprofit leaders have been established at Yale University (Program on Nonprofit Organizations), Harvard, and Indiana University, to name a few. These programs are providing not just nonprofit management instruction, but also important research such as long term studies designed to determine how nonprofits best thrive in a competitive society and in down economic times. Nonprofit educators are seeing an increase in interest in their programs, especially coming from those formerly in the for-profit sector. Through academic programs, business people can offer financial expertise and more importantly they can learn how to translate this expertise in ways useful to the nonprofit sector.

More Health Care Nonprofits Becoming Privatized

Occasionally, when a nonprofit begins to function more like a for-profit, its executive or board decides that it should become a for-profit. When a public government-funded or nonprofit hospital partners with a for-profit pharmaceutical company and the research they collaborate on becomes lucrative, the hospital might decide to give up its tax-exempt status and its focus on serving impoverished communities in favor of its profitable research component.

In the 1990s, the number of nonprofits that were converted to for-profits increased at a greater rate than any time before, with mixed results for the communities that they served. According to a 2001 Robert Wood Johnston Foundation study, "From 1992 through 1998, more than 90 private nonprofit and 17 public hospitals nationwide have converted from nonprofit to for-profit status—almost as many conversions as occurred during the entire decade of the 1980s."

While in some cases the community lost representation on the hospital boards or the level of uncompensated care declined, this study suggests that this was not the prevailing trend. In fact, some hospitals increased local community benefits without making significant changes in services or prices. The type of ownership, the researchers concluded, was less important than the local market conditions and relationship between the community and the hospital before it was converted. Moreover, researches posited that if a hospital that would have closed was saved and that hospital now paid taxes, the community would benefit.

Cross-Sector Alliances: You Scratch My Industry and I Will Scratch Yours

In the last decade, cross-sector alliances between for-profit businesses and nonprofits have boomed. Books addressing this trend such as *Nonprofit and Business Sector Collaboration* by Walter Wymer and Sridhar Samu are quite popular, and spell out how these alliances take on many forms, including corporate philanthropy, corporate foundations, licensing agreements, and sponsorships. The alliances can be complex and risky for both the nonprofit and the for-profit business, but the benefits usually outweigh the risks, and for this reason it is a practice that is probably here to stay. For the nonprofit employee with experience in the for-profit sector, understanding marketing and corporate branding is a terrific asset to bring to many organizations that are hoping to grow these alliances.

Susan G. Komen for the Cure is a nonprofit organization that was founded in 1982 by Susan Komen's sister after Susan died from breast cancer and provides a huge source of money for the fight against breast cancer around the world. According to its Web site, since 1982 it has invested over a billion dollars to find a cure. One of the foundation's major annual events is the Race for the Cure, which began in 1983 with a 5K race and 800 competing runners. Each runner raised pledged funds for breast cancer research, screening, and treatment. By 2002, over a million people participated in more than 100 races throughout the United States and in two other countries. Over the 25-year history of the nonprofit, multiple corporations have joined in the Race for the Cure through a range of cross sector alliances. Official sponsors have included Yoplait USA, Ford, REMAX International, New Balance Shoes, American Airlines, Motts, and Better Homes and Gardens. On the National Sponsor Web page for Susan G. Komen, the American Airlines entry includes the following text:

> Susan G. Komen for the Cure(r) and American Airlines have been partners in the fight against breast cancer since 1992. American Airlines is the exclusive airline sponsor for the Komen Race for the Cure(r) Series and in 1994, American Airlines was named the "official airline carrier" of the Series.

Clearly the benefit of these partnerships is mutual. The nonprofit receives large donations and other funding, and the corporate sponsors can link their brand to a popular cause. Authors Wymer and Samu reveal some interesting alliances that have taken place in recent years: Walt Disney Company has given $70,000 dollars to Habitat for Humanity to build a home in Burbank (an example of corporate philanthropy), the Ford Foundation has provided funding to the Consortium for North American Higher Education Collaboration (corporate foundation), SmithKline Beecham had an agreement that it can use the American Cancer Society logo in promoting its nicotine patch (licensing agreement), and in 1995 Nabisco created a special box of its animal crackers for the American Zoo and Aquarium Associations for sale in participating zoos and aquariums. From each box sold, the nonprofits would receive five cents (transaction based promotion). All of these are examples of mutually beneficial cross sector alliances.

Growth in Watchdog Nonprofits

The relationship between nonprofits and corporations is not always harmonious. Sometimes, instead of partnering with large companies, nonprofits pressure them to reform their business practices to improve labor and environmental conditions. In the last few decades more and more watchdog groups have formed for the purpose of forcing national and global powers to change the way they do business. For example, in the early nineties, Chiquita came under intense scrutiny for labor and environmental practices in Latin America. After much pressure and negative media attention, Chiquita partnered with the nonprofit Rainforest Alliance, whose mission is "to conserve biodiversity and ensure sustainable livelihoods by transforming land-use practices, business practices and consumer behavior."

Working with the Rainforest Alliance on "the Better Banana Project," Chiquita improved its environmental and labor practices. By 2000, Chiquita could boast that 90 percent of its bananas sold in Europe and two thirds of the bananas sold in the U.S. market "come from farms that have been certified by the Rainforest Alliance as meeting its standards for rainforest conservation, wildlife protection, soil conservation, waste management, and worker benefits."

The relationships between corporations and watchdogs are often initially adversarial. If they do form an alliance, it is often because negative publicity has forced the corporation to change its stance.

Cause Branding: When Companies Start Their Own Nonprofit Organizations

Since the 1990s, increasing numbers of corporations have been forming their own nonprofits to further causes important to the companies' owners or employees. This practice is known as cause branding. Strategic marketer Carol Cone writes on the Web site of the Public Service Advertising Research Center that "Today's pioneers are turning a concern for causes into long-term brand equity. At companies such as Avon, The Home Depot, Target, Timberland and ConAgra, comprehensive social commitments have become an integral way to conduct business and a core component of corporate reputation, brand personality and organizational identity."

In 1999, food manufacturer ConAgra (owner of Healthy Choice, Orville Redenbacher's, Hunt's, and Chef Boyardee) started the nonprofit Feeding Children Better, whose foundation Web site lists its mission as ending childhood hunger in the United States. *Fortune* magazine writer Susan Casey writes that the owner of the private company Patagonia, Yvon Chouinard, began his clothing company with the idea of giving back to the environment. That he did, Casey reveals: "In 2001 he created One Percent for the Planet, an alliance of businesses that pledge to donate 1 percent of gross revenues to environmental causes. To date, 500 organizations have signed on." Between 1985 and 1997, Chouinard donated $26 million to grass-roots organizations, and initiated his own organization Conservacion Patagonia, "a nonprofit dedicated to protection of wildland ecosystems and biodiversity in the Patagonia region of Chile and Argentina." Its main project is to create Patagonia National Park, which would be similar in size to California's Yosemite National Park. Patagonia employees are encouraged and given time off to go work with the nonprofit in Chile and Argentina.

Cause branding can pay off for the nonprofits aligned with the corporations and for the corporation itself. According to the 2000 Cone/Roper Executive Study, Americans today are supportive of, want, and expect companies to be socially conscious. In fact, "the acceptability of cause marketing has reached a high of 74 percent, up from 66 percent in 1993 . . . Having a cause program has become a 'must do' in the marketplace for companies to remain competitive."

Everyone
Knows
An Informed Decision

Considering graduate school or post-bachelor training in nonprofit management? Send out for informational material from as many different nonprofit university programs as you can, whether in your part of the country or 500 miles away. The more you have to pore over, the better chance to see what kinds of programs, classes, reading, research, and internships are out there. Many universities that have full time traditional programs also have night classes for working professionals that can give you a taste of what a program might be like. Informational sessions are also available in many regions, and you might even consider online training and programs such as Webcasts and Podcasts.

The Growing Importance of International Nonprofits

Over the past two decades international nonprofit organizations have grown in number and scope. Often referred to as nongovernmental organizations or international nongovernmental organizations (NGOs and INGOs, respectively), these nonprofits work in a multitude of ways across the world and include such groups as the Red Cross, Green Peace, Oxfam, and Amnesty International. According to Helmet Anheier and Nuno Themudo's article "The Internationalization of the Nonprofit Sector," international nonprofits work in the fields of international relations, human rights, humanitarian aid, economic development, and the environment. Some set up offices in several countries, some create federations of various national organizations to fulfill a mission, and some form coalitions with other groups in order to tackle a single issue, such as banning landmines.

While comprehensive data is not yet available on the exact growth of the international nonprofit sector in all areas, enough information is available to show that they have expanded in significant ways since the early 1990s. A study by Elizabeth Reid and Janelle Kerlin at The Urban Institute Center on Nonprofits and Philanthropy reveals that while all nonprofit areas have grown in the United States, international development and assistance organizations have grown the most rapidly, and in 2003 they accounted for 74 percent of all U.S.-based international nonprofit organizations, a 2 percent increase from 2001.

According to Reid and Kerlin, over 5,500 U.S. nonprofits operate in the international arena, which represents close to 2 percent of all nonprofits operating in the United States. A comprehensive study by the Johns Hopkins Comparative Nonprofit Project finds that the INGO is the most volunteer- and private donation-driven nonprofit structure behind churches. A large portion of INGO revenue comes from private giving, and INGOs rely even more on volunteers than national nonprofit organizations. Examples include Amnesty International, with over one million members and regular donors in over 140 countries and territories, and the Friends of the Earth Federation, with five thousand local organizations and a million members.

Official aid flowing through INGOs has increased significantly, suggesting that countries recognize the political and economic relevance of these nonprofits. According to Anheier and Themudo, "Using data on INGOs registered with the United States Agency for

International Development (USAID), the world's largest donor, we found that in just twenty years, total income of INGOs more than doubled from $2.3 billion in 1982 to $5 billion in 1992 and then more than tripled to $16.8 billion in 2001."

A Growing Role for Women and Minorities

"Don't get caught up in the wage gap," says nonprofit consultant and executive Rosetta Thurman on her blog. She continues, "Gas prices are too high for this nonsense. Do yourself and everyone else a favor and negotiate a higher nonprofit salary so we can start raising the bar for all women and people of color working in our field." Indeed, women and minorities have been involved in voluntary nonprofit organizations even before they could legally vote in the United States, and today their prospects for leading and impacting nonprofits is better than ever. According to a recent study by Bethany Sneed and Kelly LeRoux, greater numbers of women and minorities are employed in upper management in private nonprofits than they are in the for-profit sector. However, whereas women tend to earn more in nonprofits than in government jobs, the opposite is true for minority workers. Sneed and LeRoux's research makes clear that while opportunities are often better for women and minorities in this sector, there are problems that impact these groups, as well as many others. Burnout and the feeling that there are not enough people for the amount of work is one, and problems with equal pay for equal work still apply in this sector as well.

Everyone Is Plugged In

A large percentage of nonprofit organizations serve their communities with face-to-face contact and good old-fashioned letters and newsletters sent through the mail. But in an age of social networking and Internet fund-raising, technology plays a role, too. Since a variety of nonprofit groups around the United States are membership-based organizations, and even more rely on volunteers, Web sites are becoming more and more critical for reaching out to members and generating interest and donations. Savvy nonprofits develop online databases that can target people based on a variety of demographic information. These days, it seems like the whole world is plugged into the World Wide Web, and nonprofits have much to gain by taking advantage of this global communication network.

This was not always the case. As late as 2000, less than 10 percent of nonprofits indicated that they had been successful using Internet fund-raising and only 7 percent felt that e-mail was an effective tool for their organization. However, according to the *Philanthropy Matters* article "Clicking on Cultivation," in 2008 the number of groups that reported success with Internet fund-raising was around 32 percent. E-mail success had jumped to 28 percent. In part this is due to the sheer number of people who now use computers in their daily lives. According to a Department of Commerce study, in September of 2001 almost 54 percent of everyone in the United States was using the Internet, up by almost 10 percent from just the year before. By 2003, 62 million homes around the United States—or 55 percent of the population—had a computer connected to the Internet. For affluent homes, or those making over $100,000 a year, a full 95 percent owned one or more computers and 92 percent were online.

Social Networking: Potential, Problems, and Promise

Social networking is another area that nonprofits are exploring. This is not surprising, since the whole world seems to be updating Facebook statuses, tweeting, and becoming "friends" with people they may or may not know.

To look at how a nonprofit might tap into a social network's ability to generate interest, consider a fictional character, Joe Internet: A few days ago Joe logs onto Facebook and notices that a friend that he admires has suggested he join the Coffee Kids, a small nonprofit in Santa Fe. In two clicks, Joe is at the nonprofit's Facebook Causes Coffee Kids page, where the mission is succinctly described, and he discovers that not only does he agree with what they are doing but is motivated to donate. Two clicks later Joe has completed his first donation (since he already has a PayPal account, he does not even need his Visa or MasterCard number) and Coffee Kids has a way to keep Joe informed of what is happening, to send a snail-mail thank you card with more information about the organization, and perhaps solicit a second donation.

This is a common scenario, likely one you have experienced first hand if you are a social networker. However, how big a boon the Internet will be in terms of donations and generating interest in a nonprofit cause is not yet certain. According to *Nonprofit Times* writer Mark Hrywna, in the two years since Facebook launched Causes—the area where nonprofits can post their organizations' pages—only a miniscule number of people that join a cause actually donate cold hard cash to it. While the top Causes group, the Nature Conservancy, has raised $198,000 with Causes, and Causes has given very small nonprofits exposure, most nonprofits have not benefitted their bottom line substantially by being visible on social networking sites. They can, however, use them to generate interest and name recognition, and to spread their message. Hrywna reveals that over half the nonprofits surveyed in two recent large studies "intend to increase social network project staffing over the next year and about 80 percent commit at least one-quarter of a full time staff person."

The sheer number of people online throughout the day makes Internet fund-raising more of a possibility, but this is only part of the story. Nonprofits and those that support them are also creating and teaching groups how to use sophisticated programs that make Internet fund-raising much more user-friendly than in previous years. Web sites, Webinars, and articles from the *Nonprofit Times* and the Idealist.org Web sites provide nonprofits with ideas and data research to better reach their nonprofit base. The nonprofit Netaction.org provides tips for outreach and organizing online, and many online marketing experts such as Convio.com's Vinay Bhagat provide online marketing strategies such as "Optimize your Web site to convert visitors to e-mail subscribers. Target a 3 percent conversion rate of unique visitors to new subscribers," and "Use multiple e-mails in a series to lift appeal response rates. Suppress those who respond to earlier appeals in the series." In essence, good marketing strategies that have been used for years are being combined with strong user-friendly Web sites to generate new members or donors, or both.

Technology and Technology Web Sites Geared to Nonprofits

Other online resources offer even broader technology information and support. The Web site TechSoup.org offers itself as the "technology place for nonprofits" and provides articles on software companies whose products simplify nonprofit business plans, including telecommunications tools like Voice over IP (VoIP), virtual PBX, and virtual private networking (VPN). These technologies facilitate teleconferencing and telecommuting and provide affordable ways to hold offsite (virtual) meetings. The Web sites also provide numerous tips for nonprofits, such as how to convert image files (for example, converting TIFF files to JPEG) in order to publish them on nonprofit Web sites.

Possible Future Trends in the Industry

Sometimes it is unwise to discuss future trends, especially ones related to an administration that will hold power for a finite period of time, or a congress that leans one way politically for a few years but then might change course drastically after a new election. But because every once in a while they can and do enact legislation and initiate programs that are difficult to undo quickly, it makes sense to explore how these programs and government promises might change the scope and nature of nonprofits and how they operate in the United States.

Expansion of Public Service Programs

After the election of Barack Obama in 2008, applications to service-based nonprofits and federal volunteer service programs shot up. During his campaign, Obama had spoken extensively about expanding public service programs such as Teach for America and the Peace Corps, leading to a jump in both interest and applications at the beginning of his administration. According to journalist Karla Schuster, online applications for the Peace Corps alone went up 175 percent around the time of the inauguration. A March 2009 report by NPR's NewsHour Extra revealed that Teach for America had seen a 42 percent increase in applications, and the Peace Corps a 16 percent increase.

The Serve America Act, a bill signed into law in April of 2009 with broad bipartisan support, calls for a huge expansion of the number of people in AmeriCorps. According to the OHS (Occupational Health and Safety) Web site this means the number of people participating will go from 75,000 in 2009 to 250,000 by 2017. The bill provides $6 billion between 2010 and 2014 for service groups including AmeriCorps and four new corps: a Clean Energy Corps to encourage energy efficiency and conservation; an Education Corps to

On the Cutting Edge

Virtual Networking

In addition to social networking sites like Facebook, some nonprofits are exploring the virtual world of Second Life (SL), a free 3-D online world with characters created by the people who sign up to inhabit the world. Nonprofits in SL have set up islands around different themes such as Eco Commons and Justice Commons. At present, SL seems most effective as a place for nonprofit staff and volunteers to join in discussion together, to share ideas, and to promote awareness for a cause. Members can hold meetings in this virtual world, effectively cutting costs and their environmental footprint by not driving or flying to come together. Nonprofit professions meet in SL for conferences, brainstorming sessions, and to simply talk with other professionals doing similar work or who have expertise they are willing to share. TechSoup has created a Web site, Nonprofitcommons.org, which provides information about SL to nonprofits.

Another area of increased use is Twitter, the free messaging feature that allows people and groups to send quick information in real time. Nonprofits use these short message boards (140 characters or less) to inform (X group is responding to ongoing flooding in the Midwest, or Y group needs diapers donated to a specific site), to connect people to educational links, to provide timely news feeds for breaking events, to pique interest for a cause, and to see what other activists are doing.

With Twitter it is also possible to upload "twitpics" or photos, such as a photo of a dog that needs a home. Twitters are often fun to peruse and when a nonprofit does it right, it really does draw the audience in. Consider this twitter from the National Wildlife Federation: "Would You Drink Coffee Made from Animal Droppings?"

help increase student engagement, achievement, and graduation; a Healthy Futures Corps to improve health care access; and a Veterans Service Corps to enhance services for veterans. A National Civilian Community Corps will focus on disaster relief, infrastructure betterment, conservation, and urban and rural development. Finally,

INTERVIEW

Trends and Opportunities in the Aging-Services Sector

Sharon Dornberg-Lee
Licensed clinical social worker, Chicago, Illinois

You have been in the nonprofit sector for more than 20 years and at your current job for 12. What are some of the trends you have witnessed around non-profits over the years?

There is an increasing focus on accountability. For instance, our agency is now managed by people with a business background. As part of this focus comes an emphasis on what's called "evidence-based practices"—this is the buzz-phrase that's all over the social service industry in recent years—which is essentially looking at outcomes and why are we doing what we are doing. What are the best practices, not just from our idealistic kind of lens of "Gee, I really think anecdotally this is effective," but what does the research show? I really think this is not just the wave of the future, but of the present, and I think more and more it is going to be tied to getting funding.

It also points to the need for us to do research in the practices that we believe work. We need to build research components into our practices to build a case for why something is effective—otherwise [the practices we believe work but cannot show] might go the way of the dinosaur in terms of funding. In the not-for-profit world in general, there is just a need for us to be accountable for outcomes for whatever it is that we do and that's nothing necessarily new—funders want to know how their dollars are spent. People want to know how their increasingly scarce dollars are being spent, not that you just have good intentions—not just "We ran a shelter and served 30 people," but what were the outcomes in the longer run for those 30 people?

With respect to the newer business focus, what has been the response from staff like you that does direct client work?

At first social workers are sometimes skeptical of the focus on revenue, revenue, revenue, or on the increased fees for services that our more affluent clients are able to provide, but over time they have seen that this focus and the attempts at funding diversification have not changed the mission or meant that the underserved low-income-clients are neglected. In fact, because of this diversification, the agency is faring well in very difficult times where other agencies are making deep cuts. Some are now recognizing that "it's a good thing to have a thoughtful plan and a business model." For example, our agency built a senior housing development for mostly wealthier seniors. When they buy a condo in a CJE senior housing development it actually means there is more money for the indigent. So now there is more trust.

So how would you characterize the state of your particular industry?

It is very good, even at this time. Aging is a good area to be in overall. The need exceeds the talent pool. Demographically everybody knows that the baby boomers are older and there are a huge number of folks that are going to need—and not only need but want—services. I think the current baby boomers are very open to receiving all kinds of services that perhaps the older generation were a little bit more reluctant [to receive], certainly in terms of mental health services. This generation has often received mental services in the past and they are open to it and don't see it as stigmatizing. But they are also open to all kinds of services, whether it is a retirement community that meets their needs, or a social service that they need, there is going to be a tremendous need.

And right now there are not a tremendous number of social workers, or administrators who are in the field. There is a growing number that are seeing the need and entering the field, but I think it is nowhere near the number entering other fields, for example school social work, and practice settings. So there is a mismatch between the number of people who are being trained and the jobs available. So I think it is a great time to enter the field of aging and working with older adults.

Can you describe the different settings that exist to work with older adults?

There are so many: you could work in an adult day center where older adults with dementia or other issues can go during the day, a center that provides stimulation and programming during the day while an adult child that the senior lives with is at work; you could work in a residential setting or living community; you could work in a nursing home—in good resident-friendly and consumer-driven nursing homes there are wonderful opportunities; you can work in home-health; you can do what I do which is providing mental health services to older adults in their homes or in an office setting; you can go into private practice serving older adults.

These jobs involve a lot of different education levels and skills, too, right?

Absolutely. There are numerous positions at bachelor's and master's level—case management, or administration for an aging services

(continues on next page)

INTERVIEW

Trends and Opportunities in the Aging-Services Sector (continued)

organization or mental health agency. You can certainly work in a hospital setting or a geriatric unit. There are just a million different ways to work with older adults, such a host that I feel like I'm just scratching the surface. It's wide open and it's a nice population to work with.

Could you expand on that last point: how is this population a nice one to work with?
Well, it's especially a nice population for people just entering the profession. It's a forgiving population to work with. Older adults are very respectful to young professionals. I feel like [older adults] are really responsive to a kind, caring person. It's a good population not only for the more seasoned professional but as you are building your skills. You can also feel that you are making a big difference in somebody's life. A lot of the older adults that I work with are very isolated and they really appreciate whatever services you provide. Some of the graduate students that I supervise are pleasantly surprised when I tell them the range of jobs that they could do, the breadth of roles that they can play, in working with older adults.

That's not to say it's easy. It can be a very challenging population. There are a lot of challenges because you have to have quite a bit of knowledge about medical and mental issues around aging, and about other social issues.

It's also a population with a long history and they have such interesting stories. If you are in social services and are drawn to learning about people's stories, this is a great field.

an educational component will allow seniors to work in public service, earning $1,000 education awards that can be transferred to a child of the senior's choice. Not surprisingly, Americorps places its workers at a multitude of nonprofits and other public organizations around the county by providing grants directly to them, and it is likely that the new corps will likewise do so.

Tax Refunds for Wealthy Who Give to Charity

When new administrations come into power, the changes they make often directly impact how nonprofits do business, especially when they impact giving. One change that has worried nonprofits is how much people can deduct for charitable donations. The *Washington Post* writer Philip Rucker reports that one change, effective in 2011, would reduce the tax deduction for charitable giving from 35 percent to 25 percent for married couples that make over $250,000 a year or singles that make over $200,000. This would put the higher income homes on par with households below this income mark that currently get the 25 percent tax deduction. During good economic times, this may not impact what a family decides to give; however, economic times are not always good, and this tax change has some nonprofit leaders worried and skeptical. Some economists editorialize that the wealthy will simply give less, punishing the nonprofits, especially those that rely heavily on wealthy donors such as universities and arts groups.

While some feel that charitable deductions will not adversely affect charitable giving, Rucker cites a report from the Center on Budget and Policy Priorities and the Center on Philanthropy at Indiana University, finding that charitable contributions would fall by around 1.3 percent and the latter reporting that overall giving would drop by 2.1 percent. And while the 2011 tax rule might seem fair to many—why should upper income homes get a greater tax break on donations than the middle class—in a time of economic uncertainty, some inside and outside of charitable organizations are questioning whether this change is wise.

Green Jobs Offer Greener Pastures in Some Non-profit Industries

The verdict is still out for how much green jobs will increase employment opportunities in the nonprofit sector over time, since much of the government funding will go to state and local government jobs as well as private industry. However, for those working in conservation, preservation, clean energy, and other green industries that get a large percentage of their funding from the state and federal government, the outlook is good because the stimulus funding passed in early 2009 explicitly ties environmental policy to job creation. At the time of this writing, Kevin Whitelaw of National Public Radio reports that the pace of stimulus funding for green-energy projects is picking up: "The Energy Department was authorized to spend $36.7 billion, much of it on clean-energy programs. To date, however, only about $461 million has been spent and only 1 percent is expected to be spent by the beginning of 2010. But officials say the pace will really start to pick up so that by 2012 that number will go up to 17 percent."

Chapter 3

On the Job

The existing nonprofit jobs throughout the United States are diverse and far-reaching, crossing many sectors and including such dissimilar positions as webmaster, social worker, accountant, and writer. A job in the nonprofit sector can include pay as high as $700,000 dollars for executive directors of the largest nonprofits or as low as $15,000 annually. This chapter provides in-depth information on nonprofit jobs—what they are, how they relate to other jobs within the organization, and, when possible, how to move up or transition to a job that is complementary. The first subsection presents nonprofit jobs that are common to many kinds of nonprofit agencies, although not necessarily all, and subsequent sections cover jobs that are specific to the following categories: arts and media, education, environment, grant-making, health care, and social services.

Numerous nonprofit job Web sites provided key information about the multitude of nonprofit jobs listed in this chapter, including the Idealist Web site job board, Nonprofit-jobs.org, Nonprofitjob-scoop.org, the Philanthropy Journal's Nonprofit Jobs board, and the nonprofit area on Careerbuilder.com. The Bureau of Labor Statistics is also an exceptional place to discover the most common job titles, salaries, and in some cases career paths. If you want to learn more, the nonprofit job sites also provide user-friendly tools to get the job searcher to the right job category. These sites often include useful links to potential employer's Web sites. As you read through the lists of jobs here, recognize that this should be a starting point to encourage further thought and research.

Nonprofit Jobs: General

A lot of nonprofit organizations need the same types of workers. Here are some.

Canvasser/Senior Canvasser

This worker is on the front lines for environmental, conservation, public policy, and health care organizations, just to name a few, and must be well-versed in and highly dedicated to an organization's mission. The job involves door-to-door or on-the-street contact with passersby within a wide range of communities, especially in urban areas and university settings. Some canvassers are also hired to make phone calls to targeted members or potential members, as a telemarketer would.

The goal of the canvasser is to educate and raise membership or funds for their nonprofit (Greenpeace, GOTV) or to increase voter turnout around a certain issue. Another goal might be to organize a community around an issue in order to pressure for effect a change. The canvasser is essentially a salesperson for the organization. Canvassing takes a special kind of employee—one with an amazing work ethic that likes interacting with people and who can take rejection and forge on. The turnover is often high in this position.

Canvassers report to senior canvass administrators (coordinators) and other field workers, usually at a local field office. Senior canvassers may need to understand GPS systems and may also be responsible for creating surveys that the canvassers will administer. Pay for this job is often low, but a top-notch canvasser may move to a coordinator or community outreach position.

Chief Financial Officer (CFO)

In nonprofits, this position is also called chief financial and administrative officer (CFAO), director of financial services, director of finance, fiscal director, or development director. The CFO is sometimes a Certified Public Accountant (CPA) but more often has a Master of Business Administration (MBA). Many CFOs come to nonprofits after working first in the for-profit sector, although this is by no means a requirement. The CFO must have a thorough understanding of nonprofit financial management, including government grants, fees for services, earned income, foundation grants, and private donations. This director has in-depth knowledge of the operating budget, federal grants and audits, tax reporting, and financial risk-management. In the best of nonprofit worlds, the CFO is a partner and a huge asset to the executive director of the nonprofit and will spend time, often along with the board, creating a viable financial strategy for the organization to reach its short and long-range goals.

Depending on the size of the nonprofit, the CFO often wears a number of different hats, and the smaller the nonprofit the more diverse the hats. Some CFOs also must also perform human resources (HR) and information technology (IT) duties, for instance, because smaller nonprofits do not have the budget for specialized staff. He or she must work on multiple projects simultaneously, will often supervise other accountants, and needs to work closely with other fundraising/grant writing staff. According to a recent survey of CFOs by Bridgestar, "Several aspects of nonprofit culture present challenges to most CFOs, although these challenges were more pronounced for the bridgers [from the for-profit sector] than for sector long-timers. These challenges included the consensus culture of nonprofits, dealing with multiple stakeholders, working with non-financially oriented staff, and figuring out how to measure success in a culture that emphasizes mission over the financial bottom line." An effective CFO with good communication skills might eventually become the associate or executive director.

Best Practice

Stick to Your Knitting

According to Susan Wortman, an experienced fundraiser and current development director for a large health nonprofit, one of the best pieces of advice she regularly hears from her executive director is "Stick to your knitting." What this means is to go for the grants that fit your organization; do not try to make your nonprofit fit the grant just because you want it. Grants often require hours and hours to complete and staff time is too valuable to focus on a grant that does not quite fit your organization's central mission or is too small to justify the time needed to complete it. While that new grant out there might look enticing, stay with what you do best and continue to do it well.

Controller

In addition to a CFO, some nonprofits have a controller. This employee is almost always a CPA and should have an in-depth understanding of both nonprofit financial management and government contracts. A controller will often report to the CFO, focusing on the nuts-and-bolts financial issues: maintaining internal control systems in order to protect the nonprofit's assets, keeping accurate records in conformity to all regulatory standards, implementing accounting systems and measures, monitoring the flow of cash, reconciling cash transactions/cash receipts and disbursements, and helping to prepare the annual budget along with other financial staff. The controller will often advance to role of CFO or the equivalent in a nonprofit. It is useful for the controller that wants to move up to also have a master of business administration, or MBA.

Director of (Corporate and) Foundation Relations

This person develops and maintains professional relationships with the major foundations and sometimes the corporations that traditionally support the nonprofit. The job also includes cultivating and developing relationships with new foundations. The ideal employee will be an effective strategic planner and grants researcher and writer with between one to ten years experience as a foundation or government grants writer (depending on the nonprofit). The director of foundation relations reports to the director of development or the equivalent position within the agency, organization, or school and might move up to that position after demonstrated success. This director might also find that they want to use some of their skills to take on other fund raising work within the organization, such as major gifts fund-raiser.

Director of Individual Giving

The director of individual giving (also known as the individual giving manager or manager of individual giving) is responsible for increasing both the size of individual gifts to the nonprofit as well as the overall level of giving by individuals. Often working with other fund-raising staff, the director of individual giving strategizes ways to cultivate and reach existing and new donors via direct contact, direct mail campaigns, e-mail, e-news, and (sometimes) social networking. This person must carefully keep track of those individual donors who regularly give, and make phone or mail contact with them to personally acknowledge their gift. They might also be responsible for tracking donors and their gifts using detailed records and databases.

The individual giving director usually has at least three years of fund-raising experience, must demonstrate excellent written and interpersonal skills, and must be an effective project and data manager. In recent years, a director of individual giving needs to be aware of and comfortable with social networking sites and nonprofit Web sites and understand how they might be used effectively to cultivate and maintain individual donors. This might mean close contact with Web designers and other technical staff or consultants to help them best design a site that makes it easy for donors to give. This director might transition into major gifts fund-raiser, development director, or an equivalent position.

Events Coordinator

Some nonprofits employ event coordinators specifically to work on large scale fund-raising events and smaller ongoing social events throughout the year. Famous nonprofit fund-raising events include the American Cancer Society's Relay for Life and the March of Dimes annual telethon. Event coordinator job responsibilities include initial planning and scheduling of the event—be it an art auction, a dance, a rock show, or a dinner—which includes finding the best venue available and sponsors for entertainment, food, prizes, and other donations. Event coordinators often work with community volunteers to develop, promote, and run the event. They are responsible for the effective use of publicity and marketing materials and often work with a publicity department within their nonprofit, with knowledgeable volunteers, or with paid consultants. Some events may include large corporate sponsors or partnerships with corporations or local private enterprises. Events coordinators must understand the different partnerships and how they work, as well as how to develop and maintain good corporate relationships, including how to make initial contact such as cold calling. A good events coordinator can move into publicity, marketing, or other fund-raising positions, depending on his or her experience, educational background, and success as an events coordinator.

Executive Director

The executive director (also called chief executive officer, president, and managing director) directs the organization by hiring the best people and working closely with the board of directors to make sure that the organizational mission, strategic plan and policies, and day-to-day management are functioning smoothly. This CEO also must work continuously to oversee every aspect of the nonprofit, including finances, human resources, fund-raising, and community relations. An executive director is the head of all program directors, supervisors, and development and finance staff, and often is involved with at least some public relations and policy work. The director is the face of the nonprofit and, along with the board of directors, is responsible for defining and directing the organization's goals and objectives and ensuring that the services and programs are viable.

In larger nonprofits there might be an associate/deputy director that works with and directly under the executive director, taking on some of the responsibilities and functions of the executive director. The associate director supervises individual staff, program directors, or entire departments and will be the point person for overall program management, freeing the executive director to work on board development and fund-raising strategies and implementation. This position is often responsible for the coordination of all program activities and resources and a successful associate director is in good position to become an executive director of the nonprofit or of a similar nonprofit.

Fund-raiser

Charitable (including educational) nonprofits rely on fund-raisers to keep their organizations running, and this position, even in a recession, is extremely valuable. A good fund-raiser is sought after and often compensated well. If you work for a small nonprofit, you might be the only fund-raiser responsible for foundation and corporate grants, donor drives, and local events fund-raisers. For midsize to larger nonprofits, fund-raisers are often defined by the specific kinds of fund-raising that they do, including grant writer, major gifts fund-raisers and director of major gifts, director of corporate and foundation relations, director of individual giving, and events coordinators. These positions are often located within the development office in larger nonprofits and will report to the development director or CEO.

Grant Writer

A grant writer must work with the senior staff and program directors to see where the funding is most needed, then research and pursue the foundation, corporate, and governmental grants they are most likely to obtain. Grant writers must be highly organized and strong writers that can juggle and meet multiple deadlines. Grant writers and other fund-raisers are usually required to come into their positions with some computer literacy, including using Word, Excel, and Outlook. They must also be able to work effectively with the CEO and CFO, as well as all program directors. A grant writer can move into more specialized areas of fund-raising if they are in a larger nonprofit, or they can get experience in all aspects of fund-raising—major gifts, individual donors, foundation and corporate fund-raising—and take that to a different nonprofit where they can specialize in one area.

Human Resource (HR) Manager

This manager works to attract top-notch staff and, once they are hired, sees that they understand the policies and procedures of the organization. Whether the HR manager has additional staff or is a one-person show, his or her job is to ensure that the staff is working effectively and to help maintain healthy work relationships among all staff and departments. Usually this manager is responsible for managing the employee benefits program, preparing an annual HR budget, and handling complex employee relationships and training (for example, diversity and sexual harassment training). HR managers work closely with all staff and must be effective listeners, speakers, and writers.

Many larger nonprofits prefer managers to have five or more years of experience in a human resources department before moving up, and a master's in human resources may be required. The career path for someone in human resources can be vertical, moving up to head of the HR department if in a larger nonprofit, or the HR manager might also decide to transition to a volunteer coordinator position, or use their strategic planning skills to work in development or job recruitment. The job skills and educational background in HR or organizational behavior studies are often transferable from nonprofits to for-profit and government-funded agencies.

Information Technology (IT) Director

The IT director (also called a systems administrator) must maintain, oversee, and troubleshoot for all of the nonprofit operating systems utilized. Additionally, this position is often responsible for managing IT supplier relationships, overseeing and negotiating contracts with vendors, and ensuring that service agreements are in compliance. The IT manager often trains and supervises other IT staff and reports to the chief financial officer on a regular basis. This job requires a steady, patient person who is willing and able to help train non-technical staff so that they can effectively use a variety of programs. A strong work ethic, attention to detail, and an ability to simplify and convey technical expertise will make the IT director invaluable to a nonprofit.

This position is transferable to for-profit organizations and other nonprofits, and while a B.S. in management of information systems or computer science is useful, equivalent education and hands-on experience are also important. In spite of the title, this position requires a really broad range of skills—working with management, supervising other tech workers, customer service, strategic development—and someone who shows promise in these areas will move to IT positions with more responsibility and a greater salary.

Lawyers

Lawyers are employed by a wide range of nonprofits, including those that specialize in housing, minority rights, conservation, poverty and homelessness, and immigration and education reform. While some nonprofits want lawyers to come in with an expertise in a specific kind of law, such as housing or immigration, other groups want lawyers with experience in working with nonprofits and in understanding nonprofit legal issues. Within nonprofits, lawyers work on everything from researching legal issues, performing risk management and ensuring that the nonprofit is complying with legal requirements, reviewing and writing contracts, and helping to create policy. A lawyer might also be charged with providing strategic advice and counsel to the nonprofit and its board.

Major Gifts Fund-raiser

Major gifts fund-raisers cultivate relationships with large donors. At universities, these donors may be individual alumni who are carefully wooed to provide monies toward new buildings or to fund a student scholarship fund. At a health nonprofit, the donor might be a community member willing to provide money for the renovation of a low-income clinic. Major gifts fund-raisers must have excellent interpersonal skills and truly enjoy working with people. He or she will report to senior staff, which at a university will mean the director of major gifts, the university president, and other provosts or deans, as well as establish good relationships with other major gifts' fund-raisers in other departments. Importantly, the major gifts fund-raiser must have a keen understanding of how to cultivate relationships with potential donors, including facilitating systematic contact between the donor and appropriate individuals within the organization. An ability to cultivate and motivate volunteers who can then steward the donor relationship is sometimes a critical feature of this position. In some nonprofits, a major gifts fund-raiser will move up to director of major gifts or development director if they show that they have a proven track record of fund raising accomplishments, including the ability to close deals with respect to critical gifts.

Marketing Director/Manager

A nonprofit marketing director (also called marketing and publicity director, coordinator of marketing and communications, communications director) directs all marketing, branding, and publicity for the organization, including advertising (online and print), Web site traffic, and many other marketing activities. While working in the for-profit sector can be valuable experience, the nonprofit marketing manager must understand the differences in funding, finance, and culture to work effectively with others within a nonprofit. The nonprofit marketer also will often need to wear a greater variety of hats, including writer, graphic designer, and copywriter. The branding and promotion of the mission of the nonprofit is often achieved through newsletters, Web sites, campaign materials, and newspaper inserts and the marketing director should be comfortable with all of these mediums.

Often this director/manager will work closely with senior staff and technical support at the nonprofit, as well as with consultants, volunteers, and part time workers that are hired for a specific campaign or special event. A marketing director will usually have a background in communications, journalism, or marketing. In order to advance, people new to marketing might want to start at a smaller nonprofit where they can wear all of the hats, decide what they like and do best, and move to a larger nonprofit where they can specialize. This position can also move laterally to a special events coordinator or up to head of publicity and marketing.

Program/Project Directors

This position is exactly what it sounds like—a director of a project within an agency or organization. Many nonprofit fields employ project directors to coordinate the various case managers, social workers, scientists, policy wonks, and administrative staff working on a specific project or program within an organization. Community based organizations often have multiple projects in more than one area—job training, health services, child care, and housing—and each project within the agency might employ several professional and administrative positions. All of this needs coordinating.

The project director, along with the other nonprofit project directors, reports to senior staff, such as the CEO or associate director, on a regular basis and also works with the fund-raisers in order to help them report to funders about how grant moneys are being used. The program director also helps give the fund-raisers direction on what areas need to be better funded or new areas within the program for which they need funds. This position requires people with excellent communication skills and an in-depth understanding of the project they direct. Many project directors have spent years working in a nonprofit in the same or a similar program before being promoted to this position. Therefore, they are well-suited to train new staff, work with senior management, fund-raising, and marketing staff to promote the project or program, and to evaluate and analyze what is working (and who is working) and what is not.

Salesperson

Many kinds of nonprofit organizations employ salespeople (also known as account executives, directors of sales, or sales managers) to get their brand name known, bring in patrons, sell magazine or on-air advertising, and increase their client base (for nonprofits that offer fee for service programs). Sales jobs in nonprofits can be contractual—as are many telemarketing jobs—or require full time employees at junior and senior levels. Some nonprofits employ upper level account executive jobs for the seasoned marketing and sales professional. Top-notch salespeople can earn commissions for bringing in business, even in a nonprofit, and this is especially the case for those working in nonprofit health care. On the other end of the spectrum are telemarketers, who are generally paid hourly, as they are in for-profit companies, and who can also earn commissions. A salesperson must often work with a sales team to create a strategic plan to promote a nonprofit or nonprofit event or program, as well as with the financial department and senior management. Those that want to transition later to a for-profit business can take their skills with them from nonprofit sales jobs.

Volunteer Coordinator

A wide range of nonprofits employ a volunteer coordinator because so much of what a nonprofit does relies on volunteer efforts. While this job is also sometimes lumped together with another responsibility (such as coordinator of safety and volunteers) or is part time, the coordinator works with the entire nonprofit or the program directors within the nonprofit to make sure that the most pressing needs are fulfilled. A caseworker who needs a volunteer that speaks Farsi might enlist the volunteer coordinator's help in contacting community organizations, media, and schools to find someone with these specialized skills who is willing to give a few hours of their time. A special events coordinator will rely on the volunteer coordinator to help find volunteer silent auction workers, musicians, or cooks for their annual fund-raiser.

Volunteer coordinators must have exceptional communication skills and must be comfortable working with everyone from CEOs of major companies, to the board of directors, to office administrators and support staff, to community members. This coordinator is often responsible for creating volunteer policy guidelines and training materials, which may involve working hand-in-hand with the HR department. Another common responsibility is attending community events and conferences and speaking publically about the nonprofit projects and programs that impact the community.

The level of patience and good communication skills required for this position is often higher than for other jobs, as volunteers have time-constraints, might not understand the organizational mission, and may have unrealistic expectations for how their skills will be used and the time commitment and responsibilities required. Indeed, a good volunteer coordinator might move laterally or up to many positions within an agency—including caseworker, marketing associate, or human resources manager—depending on what they find that they like in their current job.

Web Designer/Manager

More and more nonprofits are employing or contracting with Web designers to develop their Web sites and make them an effective tool to get out their mission and brand. Web sites are utilized to disseminate timely information, to keep donors and members informed of organizational news and activities, and to successfully increase membership and fundraise. Skills needed include strong technical and communications ability, experience in Web construction and database development, and graphic design knowledge. Additionally, a nonprofit Web designer must show a commitment to the nonprofit's goals, an understanding of membership management and growth, and the ability to work independently and with other consultants and marketing and development staff.

Arts and Media

What do the Boston Pops, *Mother Jones* magazine, the Smithsonian, and National Public Radio have in common? They have their 501 (c) (3) tax exempt status, which is what makes them nonprofits, and they also have a variety of fascinating jobs for talented individuals. Since the seventies, there has been an increase in government and corporate funding for nonprofit arts organizations—with many ups and downs in funding along the way—leading to the growth of one sector in attractive if not always stable ways. Further, because many arts and media nonprofits have multiple revenue streams, in hard economic times they can be more stable than the ad-driven commercial media outlets. Below are some of the main jobs one will find within the arts/media subsector of nonprofit work.

Arts Director/Managing Director

An arts/managing director (also called music director, opera director, theater director, dance director, et cetera) oversees the booking and scheduling of events at the performance space, and may conduct auditions and direct performances as well. The ideal director has performing, directing (conducting, choreographing), and administrative experience and must enjoy working with a wide variety of people: performers, the board, donors, administrative staff, publicity and design, as well as the executive director (sometimes the arts director is also the CEO). The position may also include public relations, working with budgets, artist contract negotiations, and collaboration with other groups or departments that share the performance space.

Box Office /Front House Manager

Almost every performing venue requires a skilled box office manager to train and supervise workers on ticket sales (credit card payments, computer software, and customer relations), to oversee telemarketing activities and group ticket sales, and to handle customer service issues. A box office manager has top notch communication skills, can multi-task and problem solve quickly, is well-versed in booking/ticketing software, and is available to work at night and on weekends. This position might also require regular contact with the arts director and an ability to evaluate and analyze sales data. A theater or arts center might have an assistant box office position that can transition into a senior box office position. The box office skills are also transferrable to other hospitality management jobs.

Editor

Nonprofit publications, including university presses and arts programs, need editors (including assistant editors, copy editors, junior editors, senior editors, and editors-in-chief) to help compile and edit the work of the organization's writers, Web designers, or videographers. Senior editors oversee the workflow of the whole editorial department. Editors can work for an educational magazine like *Explorer Magazine* from National Geographic or a nonprofit arts organization that creates promotional materials for an upcoming event.

Editors are responsible for interacting with production and graphic designers and other editors, including developmental editors, multimedia editors, and the editor in chief of the magazine or newspaper. A junior or assistant editor is responsible for assisting the editor with screening manuscript proposals, tracking projects through the acquisition process, obtaining peer reviews of proposals and manuscripts, preparing materials for contract approval and editorial board meetings, communicating with authors about manuscript and art preparation, organizing artwork and permissions, and communicating with the production department about art and manuscript preparation. Sometimes he or she must perform routine clerical duties, such as drafting and mailing letters, making copies, and filing correspondence.

Editors often need to be well-versed in the subject matter that they are editing, and sometimes a background in a specific subject may be required. Editors usually advance from one level of editor to another—from junior to senior editor, for instance—and the more knowledgeable they are in their subject matter and the new journalism technology the better the chances of advancing. Editors may also switch between for-profit and nonprofit organizations since the skills required are not dependent upon the nonprofit status.

Graphic Designers

Whether helping with Web sites or concert fliers, graphic designers will find contract and full time work with nonprofit arts organizations. Working with marketing and communications directors and writers, graphic designers design marketing materials for nonprofits to better publicize events and the nonprofit organizational mission. Graphic designers will work to conceptualize and design posters, brochures, print ads, multi-page booklets, logos, and invitations.

A degree in graphic design or coursework and experience are usually required, as well as great communication and time management skills. Often nonprofits want graphic designers to understand Web site development and acquiring those skills can help the designer to land and advance in a job. While often these jobs are contract-based, some graphic designers for larger arts organizations will work in-house and hand in hand with Web designers, artistic directors, and other artists.

Museum Curators/Directors and Archivists

Curators and archivists both deal in preserving and exhibiting pieces of historic and artistic value to the public through museums and other public institutions. These positions are very specialized, requiring expertise in both the specific subject matter of the museum (zoo, historic site, et cetera) and an understanding of all aspects of putting together exhibitions: installation, documentation of collections, acquisitions, publications, and exhibition loans. Day to day responsibilities requires a lot of collaboration with heads of departments within the museum (for larger museums), as well as with museum technicians and assistants. Many curators and archivists must also be experts in technical features of the job, such as conservation and care of artworks or historical documents. Additionally, a curator or archivist is often called upon to research, write and speak publically about the museum collections. The senior curator is often the museum director, and someone who works as a curator can move into that position or a similar one after many years of experience and a strong track record of success.

An archivist who wants to move up might consider an advanced degree in history or library science, and sometimes this is required for any archivist. A curator often has a master's or doctorate in the subject matter, but even with these degrees the competition is rigid, so much so that a recent Bureau of Labor Statistics article suggests that "Earning two graduate degrees—in museum studies (museology) and a specialized subject—gives a candidate a distinct advantage in this competitive job market."

Performers

Art, music, and acting are specialized fields that are entered into with formal training and many, many years of perfecting skills and building résumés. Steady employment for a performer is the goal, and a hard one to achieve, whether working on a for-profit television commercial or in a nonprofit symphony. For example, while the Bureau of Labor Statistics (BLS) reveals that some symphony orchestra musicians work under wage agreements that guarantee up to 52 weeks of work, many do not have any guarantees and may face extended periods of unemployment and underemployment. Performers work with a wide variety of people, including other performers, agents, employers, sponsors, and audiences. While performers can venture into other areas of arts and entertainment, including composing and songwriting, producing and directing, an artist's ultimate goal is usually success in their specialized field.

A performer does not necessarily care or notice if he or she is working for a for-profit or nonprofit, but many musicians, stage actors, and artists do work for nonprofits because many theaters and performance spaces are nonprofit venues. Consider that several shows on Broadway are showing in nonprofit venues—including the 2009 productions of *Hair, West Side Story,* and *South Pacific.* In fact, the top theater honor, the Tony awards, are presented by the

Keeping
in Touch

The Art of Following Up

As performers and writers, you might do extensive freelance and short-term contract work. This kind of work sometimes means it becomes difficult to stay connected and network, but it can be worth the effort to stay in touch with the nonprofits for which you worked and might want to work again. Here are a couple of suggestions:

- Right after your performance or other stint, send a thank you note and let them know how much that you enjoyed working for them. Keep the note short, but make sure that you provide a contact number. You might also want to enclose good reviews of your performance or photographs that the nonprofit might put up on their bulletin board. A month or a year from now, a visual reminder could be your ticket to more work.

- If you wrote an article for a nonprofit or performed for a nonprofit charity event and would like to work for them again, find a good reason to call. For example, contact the person who loved your work and asked them if they would mind writing you a testimonial for the reference page of your new business Web site. Then write them a note back, in testimonial format, which praises the nonprofit and shows how much you loved working for them.

- If you see an article related to the nonprofit you worked for, or that might pique their interest, send it to them with a personal note. Rest assured, doing contract work for nonprofits can and often does lead to more gigs and referrals to friends in other nonprofit places.

- Ask the nonprofit if you can feature or link to the nonprofit on your business Web site or social network page. Another online way to keep in touch is to follow the nonprofit on Twitter and ask them to follow you. Then tweet about your event or work at the nonprofit and provide a link to your performance, artwork, or article.

Broadway League and the American Theatre Wing, both nonprofit service organizations. Also, there are several trade associations that support and advocate for performers, including the American

Guild of Musical Artists and American Federation of Television and Radio Artists—all membership-based nonprofit labor organizations. Among other services, these unions provide credit counseling, hospital care and college saving grants, job loss grants, mortgage assistance, and insurance premium wavers.

Technical Director

Most performance-based arts organizations need an accomplished technical director to handle all lighting, video, and sound logistics for the performances on a seasonal or ongoing basis. The technical director is a skilled worker with experience in lighting and sound editing, and this position might also include scene or set construction and design, and construction and video operations and development. Additionally, a technical director must be proficient in understanding and fixing office equipment of all kinds or supervising other staff and contracted workers in this area. Training for technical directors can be experiential—that is, by working with an expert in the field and learning the trade—or you can take classes at the undergraduate and graduate level.

Writers

Media nonprofits employ and contract with writers of all kinds— including journalists, news writers, magazine writers, copy writers, and online content writers—and with the expansion of new media forms, there will continue to be work. Whether on staff at the nonprofit, or freelancing, a writer will almost always work with copy and content editors on articles and news pieces before they are published or read. A good writer can move up quickly in a large nonprofit, eventually overseeing other writers and contract workers to put out a good product.

Education

Education is a huge field employing millions of people throughout the United States. While many educational institutions are part of the public school system and funded through taxes and federal dollars, an enormous number are also nonprofit organizations, relying on foundation money, individual donors, grants, and fees for services (tuition, for example). According to Amy Butler at the Bureau of Labor Statistics, a third of all post-secondary schools are nonprofit and nine percent of primary and secondary school students attend private nonprofit schools that are funded by tuition payments, private donors, and religious institutions.

Educational nonprofits are not just limited to schools. While many *are* schools and universities, they are also educational research institutes and early childhood through adult training programs. Additionally, this section includes jobs found in nonprofit educational research institutions. These institutes focus on a broad range of issues and therefore require expertise and training in many distinct areas—from school choice to affirmative action. When reviewing these jobs, keep in mind that Brown University, the RAND Corporation, and Jumpstart for Young Children are all nonprofits.

Administrators of Higher Education

Educational administrators (including presidents, provosts, deans, and directors of adult training/continuing education programs) manage a school or university, hiring or overseeing the hiring of the faculty and other staff and working every day and in every way to fulfill the school's mission. The president of a major university must be intimately involved in the academic mission and the financial bottom line and work closely with the board of directors (who hold the legal jurisdiction over the academic and business procedures of the school). The provost at most universities is directly below the president and shares or takes on some of the presidential responsibilities, working with the same programs, the board, staff, deans, and faculty to achieve the university's mission. This position is often called the chief academic officer.

A university or college president almost always has a Ph.D., experience teaching in the university classroom, an impressive scholarly track record, and advocacy skills—especially as a knowledgeable leader and advocate for higher education. Many people report to the president, including the vice president, the provost, the executive vice presidents, the treasurer, the vice president for communications and public affairs, and the director of alumni and university relations. Many of these positions within the university, especially the provost and deans of large programs within universities, are paths to the presidency, although the path is highly competitive and the jobs are limited.

A dean must have some of the same qualities as the university president, especially with respect to scholarly work and a doctoral degree. The dean will usually have a degree related to the program, department, or school he or she administers, and must understand and be comfortable with outreach, fund-raising, recruiting faculty, and supporting innovative new programs. Deans must interact effectively with faculty, students, staff, administrators, alumni, and other administrators. The path to a position as a dean must start in the classroom, and most deans of competitive colleges and universities were full professors before becoming deans.

A director of adult training or continuing education provides leadership and oversight for many kinds of programs and schools. Many four year colleges, for instance, have continuing education courses for working professionals that take place in the evenings and on weekends and provide advanced training in business administration, accounting, economics, human resources, and marketing, among other coursework. This position usually works with the dean of continuing education or a similar position and might be responsible for overseeing part time faculty by working on administrative and programmatic issues. A growing number of continuing education programs have an online component and require experience in online learning and teaching.

Other adult training programs may be schools unto themselves and are often referred to as vocational training institutes. While not all are nonprofit, many are and with varying emphases—from auto mechanics to computer programming to job-retraining (for example, former farm workers might take courses in culinary arts, health care, business, and even landscaping). Many adult training programs also have career placement components and the director of adult training (sometimes called the CEO) will work closely with instructors, counselors, human resources staff, students, the board, and the business community. An important aspect of the job is pinpointing those in need of services and reaching them through specialized marketing and promotions, sometimes through employers or social service agencies. Another aspect is promoting the benefit of the nonprofit to the business community in order to create positive relationships and potential future employment for training program graduates.

Finally, while government funding sometimes provides a substantial percentage of the nonprofits' budget, directors usually cannot rely on this funding from year to year and must work hard with fund-raisers to secure grants and private funding. Thus, their relationship with the community is instrumental in helping them to maintain a healthy bottom line. The directors of these programs can utilize their skills and business backgrounds to eventually work as CEOs for related nonprofits, or they can develop one aspect of their jobs, such as publicity and public relations, and use it in a different kind of industry.

Director of Admissions

Depending on the school or educational institution, an admissions job (including director/dean and assistant director/dean, admissions counselor, and field representative) is often equal parts sales, customer service, and data management. A director or assistant director of admissions at a major university or program within a university (for example, a law or business school) works hand in hand with the program deans and other senior staff to strategize how to attract the very best to their schools. They also understand and utilize recruitment models, have experience with budgets, and write and speak effectively in a wide range of settings and to varied groups—minorities, alumnae, high school students—and can develop and supervise a diverse staff.

The admissions director at an elementary or secondary school usually has a broader range of responsibilities, depending on the size and sphere of the nonprofit school. This director generally manages all aspects of the student admissions process, including establishing communication with candidates and their parents, conducting tours of the school, developing or improving the application procedures and forms, processing applications, marketing the school and working with senior staff to develop marketing materials, and representing the school at conferences and other gatherings. Depending on the focus of the school, the admissions director might need specific training in an area of expertise—a Catholic school might require this representative to have formal Catholic training, and a school that focuses on special needs might want the director to have expertise in the area of need in order to make the best admissions decisions.

Field representatives must know how to reach students (and sometimes their parents) through many avenues, including one-to-one contact, cold-calling, school/college career fairs, and leading informational meetings. Field representatives must be goal oriented and persistent, working with other regional or state-based representatives to achieve the institutional admissions goals. Travel is required for this job, sometimes many weeks out of the year including weekends.

While many top tier schools require admissions deans to have an educational background in admissions or the professional field (for example, engineering) in which they are recruiting, most schools are interested in a track record of success and experience. An admissions employee might use experience in another school department to transition into admissions, such as personnel, residence life, sales and marketing, or public relations and communications. A strong assistant director of admissions is often the best candidate to move up to the directorial position.

Counselors

Counselors advise students in many different capacities, including providing help with school schedule planning, college entrance preparation, and career counseling. A counselor for a nonprofit school usually has an educational background in school counseling or a related field, such as guidance counseling (which requires a degree in both counseling and teaching). In private primary and secondary schools, experience in the classroom and with students sometimes can be substituted for formal training, but someone with formal training is the more attractive candidate. Guidance and career counselors work with students, senior administrators, and parents to provide guidance about classes, post-secondary options, summer jobs, internships, and career possibilities.

Some counselors must provide therapeutic services and guidance for struggling students. This position (or aspect of a counselor's job) may require working with senior staff, teachers, students, parents, and other positions outside the school, such as law enforcement, psychiatrists, or mental health service agencies. A nonprofit might employ a school social worker (or contract with one) to perform these services.

A private college often has a counseling center with trained counselors to offer therapeutic services. They might also employ counselors to help with all daily aspects of student life: living in dormitories, student clubs and other activities, student government, as well as enrollment services, career and academic advancement. Many post-secondary counselors are required to have training in counseling, and may need a master's degree in counseling, psychology, social work, or a closely related field. Sometimes experience in crisis and drug intervention is also required for those working in counseling centers. While many counseling positions require advanced degrees, some positions may require no more than a bachelor's degree and experience working in residential life, or coursework in behavioral sciences and education.

College and University Professors

A professor at a college or university level has at least a master's degree and often a Ph.D. in their area of expertise. They will usually be hired as an assistant professor and advance on to associate professor before they can apply for tenure, which grants them a full professorship and all the benefits that go with it (sabbaticals, sometimes higher level classes, guaranteed employment, tuition plans for family, et cetera). Gaining a full time tenure track position at a college or university is highly competitive and sometimes takes years of working at different institutions as an adjunct professor (part time, non-tenure track). Whether at a nonprofit (Stanford, Amherst, or Princeton, for example) or public university (UCLA or the University of Michigan, for example), the tenure system requires extensive peer review to determine whether the person applying for tenure merits the title. Those who do not earn tenure usually leave within a year or two to pursue a job at another university and it is not uncommon for a professor to be turned down for tenure the first time he or she applies.

Professors interact regularly with students, other professors in their department, adjunct professors, administrative support staff, department heads and deans, and sometimes the president of the college or university. A professor who wishes to work at a research university (whether private and nonprofit or public) usually has to show proficiency as an instructor as well as have completed peer-reviewed research and writing to obtain a position and move up within the school or department. Interaction and collaboration with colleagues at other school or research institutions is also common.

While many professors are pleased to achieve tenure and stay professors, they might also transition to a deanship or other administrative positions within their university or a different one. An English professor, for example, might eventually become the dean of arts and sciences, and most deans have advanced degrees in at least one area over which they are presiding. The professor interested in moving into administration usually serves on many committees for many semesters before being considered for a deanship.

Principals

A nonprofit school might have twenty students or a thousand (as is the case with the prestigious private nonprofit Phillips Exeter Academy). The principal of a private nonprofit school is responsible for all aspects of running a school, including hiring staff, recruitment, tuition and enrollment, board development, and community leadership and advocacy. Depending on the size and funding potential of the school, the principal might have an assistant principal and deans that have specific responsibilities and report to the principal, but this varies widely.

While the principal must concern him- or herself with tuition and other funding, they also are in charge of curricular decisions and school policies. Unlike in higher education and in publicly funded schools, however, while a principal often has teaching credentials and an advanced degree in educational administration, private nonprofit schools sometimes do not have as clear an educational path. Some private school principals are priests or other religious leaders, or they may first have worked as private school teachers (but may not have been credentialed by the state).

Researchers/Experts/Fellows

Educational policy experts work in nonprofit organizations to better understand the problems and promise of the American education system and the laws and regulations that guide it. For example The Brown Center on Education Policy (part of the Brookings Institute) examines the effectiveness and success of American school curricula, as well as "academic standards and accountability, school and class size; parental choice and vouchers; and achievement gaps among racial and ethnic groups." Researchers must have expertise in a diverse area of education and no two nonprofit think tanks that deal with educational issues are the same. Many exist within nonprofit universities or as part of a nonprofit organization with broader policy and research goals, and the path to a fellowship requires advanced work and scholarly writing around educational issues that impact United States society.

A researcher might start out as a research assistant and may eventually move into a senior researcher/fellow role. An assistant conducts research, collects data, and provides basic analysis for the fellows. They support the researcher by drafting memos explaining their research, providing narrative analysis, and many other forms of communication such as PowerPoint presentations and blog entries. These functions might also be done by a research intern, often unpaid and always extending just a few months. Successfully completing an internship can lead to long-term employment and the potential for strong job references for further paid employment.

Teachers

Teachers in most nonprofit schools (preschool through secondary) are often credentialed from teacher education programs, including teaching degrees or training in specific philosophies, such as Waldorf or Montessori. However, unlike most public school teachers, a teacher at a private nonprofit is not always required to have a state credential; their expertise in a certain subject area and experience can be substituted for a formal degree.

With the exception of preschool teachers in nonprofits, other nonprofit teachers will have a bachelor's degree and may have a higher degree. Teachers train, educate, coach, and work in a multitude of ways to help children to reach educational goals required by the end of a school year. They work with the principal, with peer teachers to effectively impart the curricula, with counselors to communicate student needs or their own student concerns, and with the students' parents or guardians. Additionally, a teacher in a specialized nonprofit school such as a school for autistic children or a performing arts focus school will often have other goals that might go beyond academic requirements. Teachers act as mentors for older students, as authority figures, and sometimes as learning peers, depending on the mission or educational philosophy. A teacher can move to other teaching jobs or to an administrative job, depending on the teacher's interests and the schools' individual requirements.

The Environment

If you have been watching the news over the last year or so, you have heard the term *green-collar jobs* to describe those jobs that involve conservation and environmental protection. Indeed, the Bureau of

Labor Statistics now has a budget specifically to define, study, and produce data on green-collar jobs because the expectation is that this will continue to be a growing field. While many jobs related to environmental conservation, preservation of natural resources, and policy and advocacy work are funded by local, state, and federal dollars, an increasing number are with nonprofits. The nonprofit The Nature Conservancy employs over 700 scientists around the county and globe to fulfill its mission of protecting "ecologically important lands and waters for nature and people."

Many environmentally-focused groups employ diverse strategies to fulfill their missions, including policy and advocacy work, community organizing, and partnering with local governments and native people to fight poverty related to environmental degradation, and to conserve land, wildlife, or other animals. Not surprisingly then, environmental jobs at nonprofit organizations are often interesting and challenging, requiring a wide array of expertise and qualifications.

Director of Conservation

These directors are usually specialists in conservation biology, wildlife management, ecology, or environmental policy, or they have an extensive background in one or more of these fields. This job involves all-encompassing strategic planning, program development, advocacy, and extensive internal and external work with individuals and groups to help achieve the organizational mission. This director generally reports to the executive director or other senior management and the nonprofit board, and often must supervise and train program directors and fund-raisers within the nonprofit. Successful directors of conservation acquire the varied skills necessary to eventually become an associate or executive director (or similar position) within a nonprofit.

GIS Specialist

GIS stands for Geographic Information Systems, and professionals who know how to use this technological tool are sought after in many environmental and conservation organizations. The technology utilizes digital maps that link computerized maps with databases (GPS systems, for example, locate property lines, streams, and protected sites or many kinds). The use of GIS is so pervasive that according to Cyber-Sierra's Natural Resources Job Search board most environmental occupations require familiarity with this tool. A GIS specialist will work with other GIS experts, program directors, administrative staff, and sometimes partnering agencies (county or city governments, other nonprofit groups, or community stakeholders) to create shared digital data to further an environmental goal. Goals are far-reaching, depending on the nature of the nonprofit, and include identifying the land in a community for potential open space, analyzing the most efficient transportation routes in order for trucks to minimize carbon emissions, and pin-pointing sites of potential ground-water contamination. GIS experts are highly sought after especially if they also have traditional degrees in planning, conservation studies, ecology, and environmental sciences.

Outreach Coordinator

Outreach coordinators communicate the nonprofit's central mission by working with the public and with other stakeholders to further the organizational goals. The ideal outreach coordinator will often

Professional
Ethics

Opportunities for Advancement

Sometimes moving from one job within a nonprofit to a higher one is problematic, especially if others within the nonprofit are competing for the same job. A case manager might be competing with another case manager for the same program directorship, creating a certain amount of awkwardness or tension. The best approach to take in this kind of situation is to focus on your current job while you are at work and do the very best you can, leaving the application process, résumé updating, and recommendation-gathering for non-work hours at home. Also, if the competing coworker brings up issues related to the potential new job or shows resentment that you want the position as well, firmly let this person know that you do not want to discuss this at work, that doing so will not help you effectively do your current jobs, and that the job will be decided at the appropriate time by the hiring committee (outgoing director, human resources, executive director, et cetera).

have a background in grassroots organizing, showing an aptitude for identifying and developing outreach techniques and targeting them to a specific group—through school presentations, power points, direct mail, newsletters, and cultivating good relationships with journalists, to name a few. This position often must work to increase the visibility of the nonprofit by developing partnerships with any number of community groups or groups with like-minded environmental or conservation goals.

An effective outreach coordinator must know the organizational mission and its goals, and be able to speak and write about them. They also must be self-motivated and high-energy, know how to reach out to a wide range of people, and often travel extensively to meet with these people. Finally, an outreach coordinator must be able to work effectively with the program directors/managers to develop the most effective outreach strategies (sometimes including the Internet) and then to communicate how his or her work is going in the field. While outreach coordinators need a wide range of skills, people from many educational backgrounds can enter this field and distinguish themselves through very hard work.

Program Coordinators

A program coordinator for an environmental nonprofit usually has a background in an environmental science and may have been a staff scientist or conservation expert for the nonprofit or like organization before taking the job. These coordinators work with staff—technical experts, scientists, fund-raisers, and administrative assistants—and with senior management to further the nonprofit mission and often spend a great deal of time in the field ensuring that the program they are heading is running smoothly. Additionally, program coordinators might, with senior management, have a say in the design of a program assessment, as well as help with implementing and analyzing the results.

Some program coordinators also work directly with targeted community members, especially if working for a smaller nonprofit. An educational program coordinator, for instance, might be charged with working with local schools with other teachers to educate students about environmental service-learning projects or a specific environmental issue in the community on which students can have a collective impact. Program coordinators can move laterally to a large nonprofit and continue to focus on program coordination, or they could eventually move up to a conservation director position or other directorship within the same nonprofit.

Staff Scientists

Staff scientists for environmental nonprofits have a multitude of specialties and titles, including climate specialist, ecologist, and biologist; they also usually have an advanced degree in a relevant scientific field, although some positions might just require a bachelor's. Additionally, this job usually requires advanced research, writing, and advocacy skills. Scientists must show that they are committed to protecting the environment, and they often will work as a team with other scientists and senior staff, including lawyers. Scientists are often charged with working with local, state, and federal agencies, as well as other environmental groups and the public at large.

Grant-making Foundations

Foundations are the granting agencies that provide financial and material support to nonprofits, and most of them are 501 (c) (3) organizations. You are probably familiar with the largest foundation names, such as the Bill and Melinda Gates Foundation, the Ford Foundation, the W.K. Kellogg Foundation, or the Carnegie Corporation, but there are literally thousands of foundations around the country that employ a wide range of professionals. While some of these charitable foundations or trusts rely on one or a few wealthy funders or corporations (private foundations such as the Bill and Melinda Gates Foundation), others (public foundations) must engage in their own fund-raising in order to have the funds to distribute to nonprofit organizations. This is especially true for nonprofit hospitals and universities, and they often generate a significant percentage of their revenue through fees for services, interest on earnings and investments, and even selling goods. Because fund-raisers were discussed in the first subsection of this chapter, this section will provide information on foundation jobs that involve grant-giving.

Not surprisingly, because foundation staff might review thousands of grants every year, a common job requirement is the need for people with exceptional organizational skills. Additionally, these positions often require sophisticated data management and financial analysis responsibilities, meaning foundation staff are generally highly educated and come into foundation jobs with nonprofit experience under their belt. As you review this list of jobs, keep in mind that the Bureau of Labor Statistics *Career Guide to Industries, 2008–09 Edition* reported that over 140,000 people worked in grant-making and giving services around the country and that number is expected to increase by over 14 percent in the next 10 years.

Communications Officer

The communications officer is often one of the major public voices for the foundation in the wider community and must have excellent public relations and collaborative skills. This staff often works directly with the CEO, the development director, and other senior management to raise public awareness for the foundation's mission and goals and to help foster the public's and policy maker's desire to share in its mission. A successful communications officer usually has experience with communication strategies, media relations, and branding.

Often this position is combined with marketing and involves marketing responsibilities in order to further the foundation's mission, such as media relations, social networking, fund-raising events, and the development of foundation newsletters and other publicity materials. Communications officers must be comfortable speaking in many venues, helping to develop and implement publicity campaigns, and traveling to many different locales—around a town, city, country, or even around the world. A communications officer who wants to focus on the outreach part of their job could move to public relations and a public relations generalist can segue into a communications position at some foundations. Even someone who has spent years doing corporate PR or working as a spokesperson for a for-profit has some of the expertise generally required for a communication officer.

Grants Manager

The grants manager works with other foundation staff to keep track of all of the grant applications from beginning to end, to manage the databases, and to analyze financial reports and information. A grants manager might also be in charge of grants that the foundation is making to federal, state, and private groups, and therefore will need an extensive understanding of the grant writing process as well. In addition to experience with database computer programs (such as Excel, Lotus 123, and Macintosh Numbers) and other foundation technologies (such as Grant Lifecycle Manager and MicroEdge GIFTS) this position requires the ability to recognize strong grant writing, to communicate effectively, to supervise other staff, and the ability to manage complex timelines.

A grant manager will work with other grant managers (in larger offices) and program officers in order to verify that a grant complies with the regulations, to develop and implement the structure of grant payments, and to ensure the completion of each stage of the reviewing process. Additionally, grants managers often interact with financial staff to set grant payments and might need a working knowledge of governmental and IRS regulations related to private or public nonprofit foundations. An experienced grant writer (from within or outside of the foundation) and grant assistants or other junior managers can move into the grants management position after gaining experience and expertise. A long term grant manager can also gain many of the skills required to move up to CEO, president, or director of development.

Most grants managers and administrators have bachelor's degrees with three or more years of experience, and some positions require a master's degree in public administration (MPA) or business administration (MBA) as well. Additional requirements may include a sophisticated understanding of accounting and statistics. In 2009, a study was conducted that will lead to the implementation of a new certification in grants management. Called the National Grants Management Association certification, it was initiated in order to credential grants managers who demonstrate extensive knowledge and expertise in their field. For more information on this credential, see the National Grants Management Association (NGMA) Web site.

Health Care

Health care is a huge field with many of its jobs in the nonprofit sector. This sector includes about half of the hospitals in the United States, a large percentage of its nursing homes, medical and dental clinics, behavioral and mental health services or hospitals, and health-related positions within larger human service agencies or programs. There are also numerous nonprofits that work exclusively on policy and advocacy issues around health care, especially targeted health care: international AIDS work, children's health policy, and autism to name a few.

While some job requirements or responsibilities within this field may differ based on the organizations' nonprofit status, this is not always the case. A nurse for a nonprofit hospital will likely have the same responsibilities as a nurse working in a state-run or private for-profit hospital, yet the clientele for these different hospitals might be slightly different. On the other hand, someone with a background in nursing or medical school might be pleasantly surprised to learn of all of the opportunities to use their expertise in the nonprofit field.

Describing every job in this field is a book in itself and is simply not possible within the confines of this chapter. With this in mind, this section deals with some of the most attractive jobs that are found in nonprofit health organizations that are not directly involved with treating patients. Where possible it will highlight how some nonprofit positions might differ from their for-profit counterparts. Finally, keep in mind that many positions mentioned in the first section on common nonprofit jobs will be found in nonprofit health care organizations in general and especially in nonprofit clinics or hospitals—positions like president or executive director, development director, marketing (or communications) director, major gifts fund-raisers, human resource managers, and controllers.

Admissions/Intake Coordinator

This job is part of the field of access services. Common in hospitals, clinics, and rehabilitation/senior facilities (including Alzheimer units and homes) these coordinators along with other admissions administrative staff are responsible for getting all of the important initial information needed to effectively treat individuals or families, including preadmission, admission, discharge, and follow-up. It often involves understanding paperwork related to government health programs such as Medicaid, Supplemental Security Income, and Medicare, as well as helping the client to compile and make sense of financial requirements. Admissions and intake coordinators for health nonprofits need to understand their hospital, clinic, or organization's guidelines and also to be able to effectively communicate with a wide range of patients.

This position reports to the director of admissions and must often interact with other admissions staff to ensure continuity of service. This position does not always require a college degree, but postsecondary degrees will make advancement to a directorship or senior admissions/intake position more likely. Additionally, the nonprofit might require a CHAA (certified health care access associate) certification and bilingual skills are usually a big plus (and in some regions and nonprofits may be a requirement).

Director of Admissions

This job oversees all of the admissions/intake personnel and works with senior staff and department heads to make sure the admissions process is successful. The position might also involve arranging ongoing training of admissions personnel—in understanding government funding forms or computer database programs, for example—to help them to do their job more effectively. This position also requires trouble shooting in the form of responding to inquiries from staff and patients and relating any ongoing concerns to senior management.

Health Advisor

This senior advisor (also known as a public health advisor or health systems advisor) works with programs within a health advocacy or policy nonprofit to make sure that they are working to further the agency's mission. In addition to ensuring that the various projects or programs are working effectively, it also involves a detailed understanding of the budgets and health finance systems. Often involving an international focus, this position frequently requires someone with expertise in developing and implementing strategies to improve health conditions in a region of the country or the world. A common job responsibility is taking part in workshops and other trainings and conferences in order to share best practices among key stakeholders—partner health organizations (national or international), government program representatives from USAID or their partners, and the Centers for Disease Control and Prevention.

Most advisors have advanced degrees in public health, environmental health, allied science, public policy, or epidemiology. Because many of these jobs are associated with policy or governmental agencies dealing with national or international health issues, they are often located in cities such as New York City or Washington, D.C.

Health Educator/Advocate

Many nonprofits employ health educators to do outreach to underserved communities, providing them with information on access to health programs, help in filling out forms (sometimes in their target language), and health training in order to make better health care decisions.

This position often works closely with social workers and case managers at nonprofit clinics or multi-service social service agencies in order to understand and effectively implement outreach to the target community (homeless, pregnant teenagers, underserved seniors, immigrants, et cetera). Outreach also may involve working with other nonprofits that serve the same or similar communities such as homeless shelters or refugee resettlement programs. Health educators generally have a bachelor's degree and must be good with a large range of people, including volunteers, underserved communities, business leaders, and medical personnel. In many nonprofits, having bilingual skills is a huge plus. An effective health educator can take his or her skills in many directions, including case work, program coordination, and possibly a junior position at a health advocacy organization.

Health Policy Expert/Advocate

This health expert advocates for a specific health care issue and must interact extensively with government officials, agencies, and programs, as well as legal entities and affiliated lobbying groups. Excellent oral and written communication skills are a must and years of government relations experience is often preferred. Successful experience in advocacy is often as important as an advanced degree, although expertise in the health area is usually required, such as women's or children's health. The health nonprofit might even have a narrower focus, such as reproductive health advocacy for Latina women in the United States or improving the quality of life of U.S. immigrants living with HIV/AIDS.

Unit Manager

Many clinics, hospitals, and long-term health care facilities employ health care personnel (especially registered nurses) to support, teach, and evaluate the health care nursing and health technician staff unit within a unit. The job often involves interacting with physicians, a patient's family, and other patient providers in order to resolve complaints or clarify concerns. Thus this position requires excellent oral and written communication skills. The job might also involve hiring and disciplining employees, and authorizing daily work issues, such as overtime and break schedules. A background in nursing and usually several years experience are generally required.

Social Service and Social Advocacy

Social Services organizations are what often come to mind for nonprofit job seekers. Although health care is a much larger percentage of nonprofit jobs today, the range of employment opportunities for job seekers of all skill levels make social service and social advocacy jobs perhaps the most appealing category—especially to those just starting out in the nonprofit sector—because it includes such a diverse array of organizations. These include counseling centers, food banks, homeless shelters, immigrant and refugee services, vocational training, and community and multi-service centers—the Salvation Army, Catholic Charities, Goodwill Enterprises, and Feed the Children are just a few examples.

Social advocacy includes groups working to make positive change around a single issue or set of issues to benefit a specific community, a state or country, or an even wider segment of the population. Within this group are also the watchdog organizations (especially consumer and government watchdog groups). Some examples of social advocacy organizations include the American Civil Liberties Union, Human Rights Watch, Amnesty International, the National Right to Life Committee, and the AARP (Association for the Advancement of Retired Persons).

Campaigner/Campaign Director

Social advocacy groups employ campaigners to organize fights around a specific issue related to the nonprofit mission. For example, the Rainforest Action Network campaigner might have several campaigns to put pressure on U.S. companies doing business with banana plantations with child workers and unhealthy working conditions, or on oil companies in South America that have created environmental problems for indigenous communities.

The campaign director must work with campaigners and organizers to coordinate responses to these concerns. They must also reach out to other non-governmental organizations and shareholders to work together on these issues in order to impact the change they seek (such as a written promise from a company to change business practices). Campaign directors must have excellent written and oral communication skills and be well versed in the issues of the communities with which the nonprofit is working. Bilingual skills are also sometimes required, as are advanced degrees.

Case Managers/Workers

Most social services agencies employ case managers to work with the target community to coordinate the services that an agency or organization offers, as well as services outside of the agency. Some caseworkers are also job developers and have the specific responsibility of seeking out new job opportunities for their target population. The target community for case managers may be the newly homeless, pregnant teenage girls, refugees, seniors needing coordinated services, drug addicts, or other marginalized communities requiring advocacy and assistance. Given that caseworkers often have a large number of clients with a high level of needs (emotional, social, economic, logistical), the case manager must be patient, willing to work odd and long hours, have strong organizational skills, and willing to reach out and find new resources.

The case manager reports to the program manager and must work cooperatively with other case managers, participating in frequent trouble-shooting meetings. Most, but not all, case manager positions require a bachelor's degree (sometimes a bachelor's in social work) and some call for experience working within the target community. Often a high school diploma plus experience can be substituted for a bachelor's, although to move up to a program manager position a candidate with a bachelor's or master's degree will usually have an edge.

Counselors

Social service agencies often employ counselors to work one-on-one or in small groups with clients needing assistance around a targeted issue. This issue is often one that must be tackled if the client is to simply function in society on his or her own. All counselors require excellent note taking skills and the patience and sensitivity of a truckload of wise elders to be successful. The position will also require strong communication skills and the willingness to work with case managers, their program directors, family members of the clients, and other agencies on a consistent and ongoing basis. Knowledge of some of the social service systems and demonstrated sensitivity to the target community also is sometimes required.

A substance abuse counselor will generally have training in working with addicted clients; a residential counselor might work with troubled teens who are court-ordered to a nonprofit residential facility to learn to deal with destructive behaviors; and a financial counselor helps debt-ridden families to better manage money. Certifications and requirements differ based on the counselor position, but most require an associate's or bachelor's degree and some experience with the target community. A substance addiction counselor usually requires a Certified Addiction Counselor (CAC) certification; a residential counselor will require CPR and First Aid certifications and the ability to drive clients to appointments and outings; a crisis counselor that works with vulnerable groups will often need a master's in counseling or social work. Successful counselors can often move up to program management and in some cases eventually a senior management position.

Field Organizers/Representatives

This position coordinates a region of the country for the nonprofit by supporting member groups in a territory—through holding recruiting events, education around an issue, and sometimes activist training. The member groups are often motivated volunteers who work with others in their community to further a goal, such as human rights, gun owner rights, or animal rights.

Often the primary focus of this position is to organize coordinated regional responses to a crisis, such as a human rights violation, through public letter writing, demonstrations, and calling public officials. Another focus is to help build regional momentum around a specific nonprofit campaign or pressing issue by identifying and training local community leaders. A field organizer must have excellent public speaking and training skills, the ability to travel extensively, and the desire to work with diverse groups. Ideal candidates will already have three to five years of experience and most nonprofits require a bachelor's degree.

Social Workers

A nonprofit that calls for a social worker almost always means job seekers who hold master's in social work or licensed clinical social work (MSW, LCSW) or, less commonly, who have bachelor's in social work with experience. The social worker additionally must be licensed to practice in a particular state. Social workers work at a wide variety of social service agencies and additional expertise in a particular area of social work—senior services or child welfare, for instance—may be required.

Social workers might work directly with clients to counsel them in a number of areas or they may be hired in a supervisory role to oversee a team of caseworkers, counselors, or other social workers. They need excellent written and oral communication skills and must work effectively with senior staff, caseworkers, other social workers, social work interns, and their target client group. Compassion and a non-judgmental attitude are also required and those that consistently show these qualities sometimes will be singled out for advancement. Having proficiency in computer programs such as Microsoft Access, Excel and Word, will give the job seeking social worker and edge.

Chapter 4

Tips for Success

What does it mean to be a nonprofit professional today? It is a question that is at once simple and very complex: How does one succeed in a job once in the door? Whether working for a for-profit, the state, or for any one of the million and a half nonprofits around the United States today, there are many things to consider in order to establish a professional reputation, do a good job, and advance in a chosen career.

New nonprofit jobs can have a way of making many feel a little overwhelmed and unsure of how to do a good job. Even if you have the work ethic, curiosity, good academic and people skills, and desire to do a good job, many nonprofits give very little formal training to new job holders. Therefore, what are some of the things that you can do to start out well? Moreover, what are some of the questions you need to ask yourself to best determine if the job you have is indeed a good fit for your personality and skills?

To address common concerns or questions that often come up for the novice professional, perhaps the best place to turn is to those who have been in the business of nonprofit work for a long time—those who have stayed in the nonprofit trenches through the good and the bad, those who have managed to do both good and pretty well in spite of and sometimes because of the trials and tribulations along the way.

Sometimes the Job Description Does Not Tell the Whole Story

Ruth Ralph, the executive director of a rural health clinic in Indiana, remarks that most people do not adequately understand the different hats that one needs to wear in the nonprofit world. This is especially true for smaller nonprofits with few paid staff. If you are thinking of taking a new job at a nonprofit, one of the first things to remember is that the job description is sometimes incomplete when it comes to what the actual job entails. A good question to ask before taking a job or a new job within the nonprofit is whether you might have the opportunity to shadow a person that is currently in the job that you believe that you want. This is especially important if you want to move from one position to another within an agency or organization but do not understand all aspects of the job.

Problem
Solving
Should I Stay or Should I Go?

If a job involves constant interaction with all or some of the staff, the people likely will take on greater importance in your decision whether to take or stay in the job. A great boss can be a wonderful mentor, teaching someone new to a field all of its ins and outs, and giving them the projects and skills to grow. A boss or staff that is not supportive, a work environment that does not seem to allow for professional growth, and an office where no one is willing to help answer questions or mentor new workers are red flags that should be taken seriously.

To help determine if the less-than-perfect job is for you, consider the following questions: What role can I play in changing a negative relationship for the better? Is there mediation available when there are conflicts? Can I be effective in this kind of work environment over the long run? Do the positive aspects of the nonprofit outweigh the negative? Will the "problem" staff likely be similar in the near future? Can I honestly see myself as part of this nonprofit five years from now? Is there room for advancement in this organization as it currently operates?

Social worker Sharon Dornberg-Lee recalls that sometimes the small nonprofit is a great place to try on those hats to find out what you do best. Many years ago Dornberg-Lee worked as a field organizer for a small nonprofit office in Chicago. Beyond field organizing, her job included writing a newsletter, coordinating volunteers, talking with the media, working side by side with the executive director to develop and implement programs, and writing fund-raising materials. The ability to try many things allowed her to build unique skills and to see what kinds of job responsibilities she liked best. She eventually moved on to doing fund-raising for a large nonprofit, among other jobs, before deciding that she wanted to work more directly with clients. She then returned to school to earn a degree in social work.

While it can be scary to be asked to take on something new, it also might open up interesting opportunities. If, however, the hat does not fit, or it quickly becomes clear that you cannot adequately fulfill the stated job requirements, you should discuss the situation with your superior. Burnout is a common problem and the subject of many studies—especially for young nonprofit professionals—and your health and level of stress are important considerations when deciding whether to take or stay in a job.

Is It the Job Itself, Or the People Who Work There?

"I have never gone home from work thinking 'what's my purpose here?'" says Pamela Tims Bauduit of Clinica Family Health Services. Before taking a job or moving to a new position within a nonprofit, potential employees should be honest with themselves about the reasons for being there. Leadership and staff are a factor when taking a job—supportive and dynamic staff make the newcomer's work that much easier—but so are the mission of the organization and its structure, which ensures that when leaders leave there will be continuity in the delivery of services and day-to-day operations.

Do you really want to work for that human services agency or nonprofit hospital? Do you know and understand the nonprofit's mission? Nancy Lovett, a capital gifts officer at a private university in the Midwest with 25 years of nonprofit experience, advises that it is important to "choose the organization; don't worry about the people as much." Just like in many job sectors, in nonprofits the staff will frequently change. The important consideration is whether or not the organization is a good one, including whether it is economically stable, has a mission the prospective employee believes in, and has realistic goals for its staff.

A nonprofit organization is driven by its mission. Management guru Peter Drucker has this take on leadership and an organization's mission in *Managing the Nonprofit Sector*:

> The most common question asked me by non-profit executives is: What are the qualities of a leader? The question seems to assume that leadership is something you can learn in a charm school. But it also assumes that leadership by itself is enough, that it's an end. And that's misleadership. The leader who basically focuses on himself or herself is going to mislead . . . .What matters is not the leader's charisma. What matters is the leader's mission.

Flexibility Means Being Willing to Take On the Unexpected

How willing are you to take on new projects and responsibilities that you did not bargain for when you took your job? Experienced professionals from many areas of nonprofit work have a similar mantra: no matter what the job description they were handed during their interview, it is important to be flexible. Be like water, the Chinese proverb goes. As water moulds to its container, the wise adapt to their circumstances. "As executive director of a small nonprofit business, there is no aspect of the foundation's work that I am not involved in to some extent," says Elaine Peck of the Putnam County Community Foundation in Indiana. "My days vary greatly. I typically work 60 hours a week. I might be digging in the garden, driving an elderly donor to a function, or moving millions of dollars under new management."

Pamela Tims Bauduit, the Volunteer and Safety Coordinator for a large nonprofit health clinic in Boulder County, Colorado, suggests that new staff should take unexpected or unknown aspects of a job in stride—provided they are reasonable. Unlike the top-down corporate setting that Pam used to work in—there was a hierarchy that required many signatures to implement new ideas or programs from a chain of superiors—there is a more relaxed chain of command at her current nonprofit. This does not mean that it is less efficient, she stresses, but that every person is involved in making the nonprofit successful. And being successful means thinking out of the box and being willing to brainstorm new ideas with others. Coming up with a fresh approach to a program or implementing a new one might involve picking coworkers' brains who have other talents— like the 22-year-old that might be able to help with spreadsheets, or the administrative assistant that knows about all the latest bells and whistles for social networking sites, or the volunteer with many years of library and early literacy experience who offers worthwhile ideas for improving a clinic-based reading program. Be open to new ideas, be willing to ask for others' input, share your own ideas, and take new responsibilities in stride. If you can go with the flow and show others that you are willing to bend a little, you will usually be a valued new member of the organization.

The Role of Good Training Cannot Be Ignored

In order to be a flexible employee, sometimes extra training is needed for some tasks. Many nonprofits provide this training, understanding the importance of investing in the staff in order to build their skills and confidence to take on diverse tasks. One area that is increasingly important is fund-raising. As Todd Cohen writes in the *Philanthropy Journal*, "With the [2008–2009] recession putting even greater stress on a workforce already expected to do more with less . . . nonprofits are looking for ways to equip employees with the skills and know-how they and their organizations need in a rapidly changing marketplace." If an employee has good fund-raising skills today, they will likely advance in their jobs.

Understanding that a well-rounded staff helps with staff quality and retention, many nonprofits invest in good training programs to help attract the best talent. However, an employee asked to take on a particularly challenging assignment without being given guidance should not be afraid to inquire if training or training funds are available. It is better to be honest up front about lack of expertise or confidence in a given skill than trying to tackle something you truly do not understand. Even if there is no official training, there could be someone to mentor the employee through the process—to answer questions about a grant proposal, or to help to edit a public service announcement. Flexibility is essential to most nonprofit jobs, but flexibility sometimes requires that the muscles are trained to bend a certain way. Without it, the process will be painful.

Persistence and Risk-Taking

In many nonprofit jobs, asking others for money or donations of time or material goods is par for the course during any given week. Or you might need to help a client find an apartment or job. If the economy is bad, asking is never easy. Besides, you probably hate rejection. Everyone hates rejections, you realize, but how to get over it and move forward?

For most client-centered nonprofits, it is important that you take some risks even if this is not your nature. People who work to place clients in jobs, for instance, will spend a lot of time talking to human resources departments to see if there are any possibilities for employment and may need to do cold calling to establish a first contact. Beyond the initial contact, a case manager will then want to have a face-to-face meeting with the contacted person.

According to Lutheran Community Services' self-sufficiency coordinator, Mohammed Maraee, e-mails and talking on the phone can get you the appointment to help get jobs for clients, but seeing someone face to face is "the real deal." In a struggling economy, he adds, this is difficult, but this contact is a start because it means that four months from now the human resources departments will likely remember you. Even if the payoff is not immediate, it is important to make contact. "Most of us are visual; we need to link people with the face and name."

What is appropriate for Maraee is also appropriate for a fundraiser contacting a potential donor, a media professional trying to get an article in a magazine or paper in order to promote an agency program, or a development director looking to establish a corporate alliance with a local food company. While today might not be the right time, tomorrow or next week the company might be have a need that the nonprofit can fulfill.

Listen, Pay Attention, Show Respect

It is difficult to step back and be humble about what one does and does not know. After all, those attracted to nonprofit work often are innovators and come in with tremendous enthusiasm and brimming with ideas. For some novice nonprofit employees, starting a new job can bring out the impulse to act as if every thing is clear and that all is just fine. To be successful, however, it is crucial that a newer employee stop talking for a minute and let others—mentors, executive directors, board members, the administrative staff, non-profit experts, even experienced volunteers—provide their words of wisdom.

Listening is important in formal and informal settings. When Susan Wortman was hired as the development director at Clinica Family Health Services—a series of clinics serving underinsured and the uninsured in Colorado—she did not have a lot of experience in grant writing. The agency immediately sent her to a one-week grant writing workshop in Los Angeles at the Grantsmanship Center, which gave her the nuts and bolts of writing a good grant. Wortman remarks that it is important to remember that you do not have to reinvent the wheel—there are many free and low-cost workshops in her field that she can attend, for example. In her case, she stresses the importance of listening carefully to what the funder wants in a proposal, and then giving it to them without all the extra bells and whistles.

To better understand her new role, she also tagged along with the executive director on tours of the clinic facilities along with the agency's other guests. By being in the audience, she was able to see the clinic, in a sense, through the guests' eyes—something extremely important for a development director charged with giving talks throughout the community. Finally, Wortman says she often asks to attend meetings just to gather information about a particular aspect of the agency that she might not fully comprehend, commenting, "I may not have a lot to say, but I have a lot to hear."

Social worker Sharon Dornberg-Lee adds another angle to the importance of listening, commenting that long-term professionals in the nonprofit sector may struggle with younger nonprofit profession-als because sometimes they "don't know what they don't know" and are not realistic about the organization's resources. Recognize that there are people that have done this work for a long time and that there are things that you can learn from them, she says. Be aware that change does not happen overnight and that when you approach others with opinions or ideas you should have a sense of decorum and show respect. She adds that while it is positive that younger pro-fessionals are often assertive and are generally unafraid to share their ideas, there is a right and wrong way to go about sharing opinions.

Another perspective on younger nonprofit workers comes from the young professionals themselves. The *Chronicle of Philanthropy* recently wrote about how staff members that are under 30 frequently are frustrated by low salaries and their ability to be taken seriously by middle and upper management. According to "What Can Charity Leaders Learn From Their 20-Something Employees?" young workers need to be heard because this generation is truly bursting with new, innovative ideas. They also are having a difficult time paying student loans, and living on $30,000 a year does not go very far in most parts of the country. Additionally, some young professionals feel that any movement upward is blocked and want to know how to gain the skills to move laterally so that they can ensure that they have meaningful jobs. Finally, all evidence points strongly to the fact that the under 30 crowd is truly committed to service. As Robert Egger, founder of DC Central Kitchen, puts it, young nonprofit professionals "need a solid wage, but of equal value is a job where they really feel they have contributed. Never underestimate the power of this drive, but do not overestimate how long they will work if they are not in the process of divining the shared path."

Extend Yourself

Today, more than any time before, there is an enormous array of human and material resources available to those beginning a career in the nonprofit sector. At the 2008 Young Nonprofit Professionals Network conference, one group of panelists suggested that nonprofit professionals new to the sector should "Identify Mentors—let yourself be vulnerable and admit your weaknesses" to someone who might be able to advise you. The panelists also stressed the importance of cross-training, or building new skills by training in other areas of nonprofit work. A volunteer coordinator might spend time learning about writing grants, either with the help of a fund-raiser on staff, or on their own by visiting any number of Web sites with articles or links to articles that provide tremendous information. The webmaster may be a crack technical person with great graphic design skills, but might not fully understand the organization's goals and how they should be presented without talking to others. Likewise, a caseworker interested in transitioning to program management might take a class that deals with organizational and community-wide issues or ask a trusted superior for advice on how to go about transitioning to a new role.

Elaine Peck, the executive director of a small community foundation, started in social work over 30 years ago. During graduate school in social work at Indiana University, she took classes that dealt with both micro- and macro-level issues. Many who want to be social workers would focus on the micro-level classes, but the macro classes dealt with community and system-wide issues that captured Peck's interest and attention. She goes on to explain to Career Launcher her job progression after graduate school from social worker to director of a foundation:

> I worked in juvenile probation and developed an intensive program that provided an alternative to youth being incarcerated. I worked with at-risk families where there had been findings of abuse and neglect and at the Salvation Army Harbor Light Center with the homeless and addicted, where I moved from being an inpatient counselor, to being an administrator overseeing all the programs. My passions and interests and value system have always been focused on making a difference. As a social worker, you learn about how systems affect life and people, and over the course of my career, I have been intervening in increasingly larger systems.

One reason Peck had the opportunity to move to a new job was because she was mentored by a board member, a retired vice president for Blue Cross Blue Shield who worked with the Salvation Army. This mentor was someone who saw something in her that he felt would do well in administration—her endless energy perhaps, or strong communication skills, or her attention to detail. This was not a formal mentorship, she stresses, but adds that there is nothing like it for helping a young professional develop skills and confidence.

The combination of training and mentoring helped Peck to be where she wants to be at this point in her life. Whereas 30 years ago the formal training for nonprofit work often took place at conferences and on brick-and-mortar campuses, today a nonprofit professional has access to numerous other resources as well—Webinars, social networking sites that bring people in similar fields together, organizations like the Young Nonprofit Professionals Network (YNPN) that are designed to help people new to the sector, and night and online classes at a growing number of universities that offer courses for nonprofit professionals at all different levels.

As Peck stresses when asked what she would look for if she had to replace herself, "People have to be willing to extend themselves." For instance, Peck had to learn about investments in order to run a community foundation, and had to be willing to allow others to teach her. Sometimes this boils down to sitting down after a very long day and reading up on the areas in which the employee is weak; and sometimes it means seeking out the coworker that might help to grow the skills needed to have success in a given job.

Extending oneself is also a form of job protection. More and more people from for-profits have been enrolling in nonprofit management programs because of job cuts in their sector or because they have become disillusioned with the corporate world. Nonprofit employers might want a for-profit business manager's financial expertise, but they also need that business manager to understand how a nonprofit works. This may be important for the professional already on the nonprofit job as well, especially if he or she hopes to advance.

Extend? Yes. Overextend? No.

For those new nonprofit professionals engaged in working with clients, it is tempting to want to say "yes" to all of their needs. Client requests can be so incredibly large—and their frustration and pain so hard to watch—that you nod "yes" to helping them with something that your agency or your position is not responsible for, and that may be difficult to fulfill. Your intentions might be good, and you might honestly believe that you can scrape together resources for them, or you may ask favors of other staff that you think just *might* be able to help. While the road to hell may not be paved with your good intentions, the road to burnout and exhaustion, not to mention irate coworkers, will be.

According Bruno Sukys, the refugee resettlement director at the International Institute of Rhode Island, "Know the limits of your program. Sometimes you might have to say no, and if you do not, you might be overpromising what you or the nonprofit can do. Better to be honest." Sukys adds that while it is important not to misrepresent what you can do, you can give clients options. For instance, he often has meetings with other caseworkers during which they determine what options #1 and #2 are. "If there are no options, you give them an option called H-O-P-E. Let them know that while there might not be anything for them now, down the road, X, Y or Z might be possible." Such is the case for many refugees seeking visas or permanent residency status. If their cases have anything that might slow down the process—an arrest of any sort, or if they came to the United States without documents—it is almost impossible to help them with the immigration paperwork and the process is extremely slow. But he always lets them know that if immigration reforms happen down the line, they have a shot.

Collaborate, Cooperate, and Communicate

Sukys also emphasizes that human service workers should know the system and how to cultivate relationships with the key people and groups inside and outside of the nonprofit that will help them to help their clients. For him, that means regularly talking to other organizations that offer similar or complementary services, as well as government agencies and key people who may help. While over-promising leads to burnout and sometimes angry clients waiting for you to fulfill requests, the more people and groups you know, the more options you can give your clients.

Whether a nonprofit employs three paid professionals or three thousand, the importance of collaborating and cooperating with other staff, volunteers, and even the board cannot be overstated. Nearly every experienced nonprofit professional interviewed for this book stressed the importance of working well with others—it is a top priority when they hire, or would be if they were to be charged with hiring others.

While some people work well in groups, and some people are clearly better "people persons" than others, most nonprofit employees have to exert an effort to truly cooperate with a wide variety of people—coworkers, clients, technical staff, the board, and volunteers—and there are always going to be difficult personalities. In terms of staff performance, nonprofits often do not operate the same way as the private or public companies next door. While for-profits may stress collaboration, many stress competition just as fiercely: To succeed is to outperform a coworker; to succeed is to sell more than the next person; to succeed is to help support a company's bottom line. For the nonprofit professional, the financial bottom line is clearly important, but only insofar as it allows the organization to better fulfill its central mission.

Job descriptions frequently have the words "team player" and "excellent written and verbal communication skills" as stated requirements—and they mean it. Most nonprofits are process oriented and consensus driven, not profit driven. Consensus-driven environments can be exciting to work in because the person who has been at the nonprofit for a week and the 20-year professional

both might get to have a say in the organization's strategies and programs. However, these types of organizations can be messier than
their top-down counterparts, and they often require patience on the
part of the staff. To be effective is to remember to listen more than
you speak when dealing with other staff, to be deliberate enough to
take good notes during meetings, to ask relevant questions, and to
be astute enough to see where coworkers' strengths lie and how they
complement one's own.

Professional
Ethics

Internet Policies

Just when you think you are getting the hang of your
job, an ethical situation might come up that puts you in
a very uncomfortable position: observing a coworker that
spends a big chunk of the day surfing Web sites that are unrelated to the job, or being included in the circulation of a crude or
blatantly sexist or explicit group e-mail, for example. Before going to
your superior or confronting your coworker who sent the e-mail, you
should find out whether your nonprofit has a clearly defined written
policy that applies to the situation. If you determine that there are
strict and clear written policies that the coworker should know and
understand, the next step could be to go to the human resources
department or your immediate superior. In the case of the e-mail,
you first might want to approach the coworker and remind them of
the policy or let them know in a non-confrontational way that the
e-mail is offensive to you. Use your instincts to help you determine
if a personal conversation will be useful before making a formal
complaint. If this coworker is someone who has offended others in
the office, chances are good that you will already know this piece of
information.

If there are few or no policies that deal with Internet use in the
office or the circulation of e-mails, write a note or approach your
superiors and suggest (diplomatically) that it would be very useful to
have them. If you do not feel like these concerns are taken seriously,
be persistent but remain tactful. This will protect you and your job.
Also, be sure to document the entire process—save e-mails and write
down all related notes, dates, and times.

Examine Your Biases and Deal with Them

To be successful in a job requires one to examine personal biases or presumptions about coworkers, clients, or volunteers. It is not unusual, for example, for a nonprofit like Catholic Charities to employ people with many different religious beliefs, including atheists. A new employee expecting the staff to be 100 percent Catholic might be in for a surprise and must be willing to accept that Jews, Muslims, agnostics, and Protestants could also be working in the same department or in the same program.

That does not mean that most employees will spend on-the-job time promoting their belief systems. Indeed, there are often policies that set parameters for what kinds of discussions are permissible or encouraged during work hours. But for some it can require a conscious effort to be aware of how to conduct meaningful and respectful conversations about belief systems when it is necessary to the job. This might involve becoming familiar with other faith's dietary needs or restrictions when planning lunch meetings, understanding another groups' holidays and holy days, or becoming aware of religious practices that might take place before a group meal or in a break room. Indeed, collaboration with others on the job can be enhanced by understanding and learning about other religious practices, especially if, for example, a staff is working with people from traditionally Muslim countries, or an elderly population that is primarily Jewish.

The key to contributing to a healthy work environment is anticipating that there will be a variety of differences on many levels, and then thinking through the best ways to approach them before coming to work. It is also important to remember that others are in all likelihood working at the nonprofit because they believe in its purpose and mission.

Tips for Job-hunting and Interviewing

Whether you are going for your first interview, or are considering switching jobs within the nonprofit sector, there are a few things to keep in mind when interviewing for nonprofit work. First, in a tight economy and at a time when many people from corporate America might be competing with you, it is crucial to do your homework. Develop an understanding of the differences between for-profits and nonprofits. Read up on the industry and your potential new employer in particular. Most nonprofits today have some presence on the Web, and many Web sites can help prepare you for the interview and aid you in understanding the industry as a whole. If you wish to work for a conservation group or health care advocacy organization, find out all you can about it, as well as about similar nonprofits that do complementary work. Recognize what makes the organization a 501 (c) (3), and how your desired job relates to the overall mission of the nonprofit.

Second, if you do not have volunteer experience and you are new to the field, consider enrolling in a course that might make you a stronger candidate before you apply. Alternatively, do some volunteer work before applying for jobs. Many nonprofit jobs go unadvertised or are advertised in professional publications you may not be familiar with. This makes forming connections with nonprofit professionals—through attending conferences, volunteering, and taking the initiative to set up informational interviews—a crucial part of landing a nonprofit job. Through an informational interview, for example, you might discover that there are a growing number of well-funded jobs in the senior services sector in your geographic area, and that your skills translate well into a management position there. Informational interviews provide the job-seeker with answers to questions that he or she may not have known they were looking for.

Third, if you do have related experience, play it up: relevant community and volunteer experience will make you a stronger candidate. If you wish to work with the developmentally challenged and you spent college breaks volunteering for the Special Olympics or working at a nonprofit camp, do not forget to include this information. If you are applying for a position that involves working with the homeless and you have experience volunteering for an agency that provides services to veterans, make sure to include this information even if it is not exactly the same target group. Recommendations from a volunteer coordinator extolling your people skills will indeed translate from one field to another. In fact, bring in three references and at least two letters of recommendation even if they are not required of you when you come in for the interview. Presenting these along with your résumé will provide that much more information from which the employer can make an informed decision.

Fourth, if you hope to switch jobs within your nonprofit, make the effort to learn the ins and outs of the new job, and make sure that this job is something that will challenge and inspire you for a long time. Take the time to ask coworkers thoughtful questions and

Best Practice

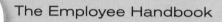

The Employee Handbook

Sometimes the simplest things are the most overlooked. When someone begins a nonprofit job, he or she often has many different things to juggle—workshops, meeting new staff, and time-consuming tasks that need to be done yesterday, just for starters—that little time is spent on the employee handbook that the employer provided. Yet this document offers the organization's policies and procedures that can save the employee valuable time trying to grasp their new job.

If the employer fails to provide a handbook, the employee should ask for it, even if he or she has been on the job for a while. Although an employee might see similarities between a previous job's handbook and the present one, he or she should recognize that not all handbooks are the same; what was permissible at the last job might be prohibited at the new one. Moreover, when a nonprofit issues an updated handbook, it is prudent for employees to look through it again as a refresher and to make sure that they do not have any questions. If the nonprofit does not have written policies and procedures (as might be the case in a very small nonprofit) the employee should speak with his or her superior to find out specific information, such as the health and safety regulations, the code of conduct, and privacy policies. This will not only make the employee better able to do the job, it can provide job protection.

confirm that you are able to do the required tasks before moving forward. Grant writer Lisa Marie Cramer, who works for the International Institute of Rhode Island, points out that for those working in human-service nonprofits, most jobs will involve direct client work. If you move to client-based work from a job such as grant writing—which sometimes has little or no direct interaction with clients—be sure that you are ready to make this major switch and that you understand what it entails.

If you are moving from an administrative job to a community-based position, as Teresa Jacobsen did when she became the volunteer coordinator for Lutheran Community Services, be sure that you have a good relationship with the staff with whom you will need to interact. Jacobsen remarks that in addition to finding volunteer tutors through Web sites like Craigslist, many of her volunteers are refugees who were suggested by case managers. Her relationships with case managers help her to find the right people; it also helps that she developed relationships with other staff through her previous administrative role. Since cross-training is sometimes lacking at a nonprofit, developing relationships that help you to understand the other jobs within an organization is critical to job success.

Fifth, when you are at an interview, make sure to answer the questions that are asked. Just as funders want specific and concrete responses, so too do interviewers. Bruno Sukys shares that when he interviews a job candidate he really *does* want to know what the candidate sees him or herself doing in five years. This is not a throwaway question for him; it provides him with insight into how serious a candidate might be about nonprofit work. Anticipate this question and be prepared to articulate clearly why you want the particular job that you are applying for.

If you have done your homework, you have learned about the position being offered and how it relates to the rest of the organization. However, if some aspects of the job are not clear, come prepared to ask questions, and listen carefully to the interviewer's answers. In addition to thinking about the impression you are making, make certain that the organization is the right fit for you. In tough economic times, of course, this is not always possible. But if red flags go up—about the organization's success at keeping staff or funding, or anything else that your instincts tell you might not be right—pay attention to them.

Finally, never forget that nonprofits rely on grants, governmental funding, fees for services, and other revenue streams that can change from year to year. Your potential new job may depend upon how well the organization interacts with various funding sources. In fact, the position might be paid out of four, five, or six different grants. It is complex and you should never forget it. If you find out the funding for the job you want is year to year, or relies on funding that could disappear very soon, you might want to reconsider. Helping to scrounge up your salary while doing your job might not be in the job description, but it has been known to happen. Do not be afraid to ask up front how the job is being funded.

The Nuts and Bolts

In a sector as big as the nonprofit one, it is tricky to talk about the day-to-day workings of the nonprofit world and how to manage them. What is true for a caseworker might not apply to a museum archivist, marketing associate, or doctor. Yet some basic guidelines and strategies can be applied to many, if not all, jobs. This section delves into the concrete aspects of many nonprofit jobs and how to successfully approach the day-to-day management of time and tasks.

Keeping Up with E-mail and Phone Messages

In this age of immediate electronic communication, keeping up with e-mails and phone messages is essential in order to avoid getting drowned in a matter of days or weeks. Do everything in your power to manage the paperless work. The successful employee must learn how to efficiently scan and prioritize e-mails. According to Ruth Ralph, e-mail has complicated her life as executive director of a small nonprofit because e-mailers usually expect immediate responses. Others interviewed state that they make it their own policy to not let an e-mail go unanswered for more than two or three days.

Fortunately, many e-mail programs have ways for you to prioritize unanswered e-mails so that they do not fall further down your inbox until they disappear from the page—and your memory. If your e-mail program does not allow this, create a document for your desktop that helps you to remember the calls or e-mails in the order of importance or urgency. This will protect you and keep the message senders happy.

Another problem that can arise is when the recipient states that they did not receive your response. To help avoid confusion, always copy yourself when you respond to an e-mail. You can also ask for a quick confirmation from the recipient in order to know with certainty that your response did not end up in their junk folder. The same applies to leaving a message on someone's answering machine—make sure the customers or clients got the message by phoning them again later for a quick confirmation.

A good way of ensuring time to talk to clients or patients is to give them a period of time when you are free, and then—by all means—make sure that you are there. Provide this time in your schedule every week. Sukys and the caseworkers that he supervises have as policy that they will each provide an afternoon a week to take walk-ins and answer questions. This helps to keep them on schedule and lessens problems if clients want to go beyond their scheduled appointment or discuss unrelated matters that are not urgent.

Susan Wortman relates that e-mail management might mean calling a meeting with others in the office to strategize how to handle a nonprofit's internal e-mails without becoming completely overwhelmed. It helps to have a subject line with a date and level of urgency, she relates. It is also important to have the right people on the e-mail lists and to make sure that the responses either do or do not go out to the whole e-mailed group. Spending time upfront dealing with this can save untold time in the end. Additionally, as Sukys suggests, let all clients and others know that it might take you up to two or three days to respond to pertinent e-mails; many have needs that must be addressed and the clearer you are about this, the better you will assist your clients.

Be Specific, Know Your Numbers, and Get Organized

Once upon a time, grant proposals and official staff reports (to a superior or the board, for example) were filled with touching stories about the wonderful organization or program within it. No more is this the case. If reports and grants are a large part of your job, you probably already know that funders and the government or other agencies want specific information, that they provide little space to give that information, and that they demand cold, hard facts. There are a lot of nonprofits out there with needs, and the funders and hierarchy want to see how, exactly, your organization is fulfilling its stated mission in the most effective and efficient manner.

Former fund-raiser Sharon Dornberg-Lee, who today works as a social worker, believes her specificity is one reason she often got the money her organization asked for: "I've had success not necessarily because I'm a good writer, but because I was very specific when I answered how the funds were going to be used and I worked with the program directors to make sure that they had thought through how they were going to use the funds." Development Director Wortman also stresses that when you provide concrete numbers in relationship to a project, the potential donor can get a strong and realistic idea that "with X dollars you can fund prenatal care for five babies."

She further emphasizes that it is crucial to write reports or grants "in English, not technical language" so that the funders understand what you are trying to convey.

International Institute's Lisa Marie Cramer suggests that it is wise to print out online information about grant and report deadlines and keep them in plain view. "Take time each week to put the all deadline information into a Word document and then have a really good time crossing completed tasks off the list." Cramer must complete close to 55 grants every year, which means almost one each week. Like Dornberg-Lee, she emphasizes that it is not so much that she is a good writer; it is more that she knows how to take the data and present it clearly in the reports and that she is careful to tailor the information based on the questions asked. Cramer adds that not only does she make lists to keep track of funders' deadlines, but she also puts when she will make her coming week's to-do list on her calendar. "You have to want to be organized," Cramer says, and her table full of lists with elaborate cross-offs speaks even louder than her words of advice.

The Little Things Matter

Just like your grandmother may have told you, saying "please" and "thank you" go a long way toward building successful relationships. This applies to coworkers, community members, board members, clients, volunteers, mentors, and donors. Capital Gifts Officer Nancy Lovett states that one of the best ways to say "thank you" is by sending a donor or potential donor a postcard through good old-fashioned snail mail. So few people receive hand-addressed and personalized mail any more that it is a memorable and effective way to establish or continue an important relationship. Include a personal message in the card, as well as your phone number and other contact information. Unlike an e-mail, a carefully-selected card might stay up on a donor's bulletin board for several months, serving as a reminder of your organization with an easily accessible contact number. "We aren't born philanthropists; donors are grown," says Susan Wortman, the development director for Clinica Family Health Services.

Wortman suggests that when you do use e-mail to contact donors or funders, attach photographs, such as one of a group of children enjoying toys provided by a donor, for example. Photographs can be inspiring to the donors and volunteers, and a visual might compel them to continue to think about your organization's needs. It is also

Keeping
in Touch

The Whole Story

While funders might not be interested in the story your nonprofit can tell, the nonprofit's target community and the individual donors that may contribute most certainly are. According to a recent article by Staci Jones in the *Philanthropy Journal*, "Most nonprofits market their mission only. Sure it's the driving force of the nonprofit internally, but it's not the message donors, customers and volunteers need to have to understand the organization. These audiences need to hear the emotionally compelling impact a nonprofit is having on the community. That's what makes certain nonprofits stand out in the crowd of thousands in the United States. Nonprofits have great story-telling ability and need to capitalize on it."

relatively easy to do and the recipient has the option to read or delete e-mail at their will.

Dress to Show Respect

If you are a canvasser for Greenpeace, your daily attire is going to be a tad different than if you are a marketing director for a major nonprofit hospital. Given the vast differences in the kinds of jobs in the nonprofit sector, it is very important to know your organization's dress code, if it exists, and to adhere to it. In difficult economic times, people often begin to dress more formally in the workplace, indicating with their clothing that they are serious and professional.

Obviously, for someone who works in a food bank, a straight skirt and heels or a Brooks Brothers suit would fall under the category of overdressing. However, if at all in doubt, overdress or ask your coworkers and supervisor what is acceptable. For some customers, clients, donors, or community members, it is an indication of a lack of respect if you present yourself in faded or torn clothes, or with loose, sloppy hair. This might be true for those serving seniors or people from countries where formal clothing is expected in a workplace.

INTERVIEW

One Perspective on What It Takes to Make It

Bernie Kosberg
Executive director of Ramapo for Children, New York, New York

When you interviewed with Ramapo for the executive director position, how did you know it was the right place for you?
I saw a great opportunity to use experiential and recreational activities—canoeing and hiking, living within a small residential setting and having lots of opportunity to interact with caring college students—to allow kids to blossom and get a sense of themselves. This program develops self-reliance and provides them with opportunities to relate and to develop relationships with young adults on their own and to grow. By learning how to build relationships, by learning how to be willing to participate and be willing to ask adults for help, they'll be able to feel that they have a place and hopefully they will transition to independence and work. While some might always need supervision through a group home, or a supported living situation, most learn that they can do [many things] on their own.

What is a typical day in the life of a nonprofit camp when a camp session is going on?
Over the last twenty years and especially the last 15 to 17 years, a lot of my time has been spent developing the programs that supplement our summer camping program. We also have a professional development program called Ramapo Training that provides "here and now" skills for teachers, youth workers, and houses of worship. We hire staff and we work with parents to implement a model program that we have developed—managing difficult children and building an inclusive environment.

Additionally, we have developed some curriculum materials that are very useful in schools and especially in inner city schools. We work with teachers and staff and teach them how to manage behaviors, and we also work with parents by helping them to understand and work with children on the autism spectrum. That's something I do as well during the summer is go back to the city [NYC] and work with our youth service and education trainers to document what we do, and to develop comprehensive manuals for curriculum.

Another part of it is ensuring that this campus is a campus that serves the children well, that the activities are structured. We do studies to ensure that the activities are benefitting the kids and the ways we work with kids are beneficial. If they are not, we use the information that we learn in our studies to modify that. We're also very involved in training staff; we need to have staff that understands what their role is in working with special needs kids. The staff learns how to look at the world through the children's eyes. Many of these kids are overwhelmed by life's experiences and may not be open to intervention. So a large part of my time is spent training staff [around that] as well.

I also spend my time supervising the senior camp leadership. With 220 kids and 275 staff during the summer camp program, I surely couldn't do it on my own. There are about five or six senior staff and we have frequent meetings and I supervise them to make sure that we are all on the same page; that we all agree with our strategies in terms of working with the kids.

Additionally, a lot of our time is spent working with parents and helping them understand where our programs are. [We need to have parents share information] because we know that parents have a much better understanding of some of their youngsters' patterns and behaviors.

So if you put all that together, the work with the parents and supervising staff, ensuring that the buildings and the grounds are the best that they can be—are inviting and really kid-friendly—that kind of fills up my day.

How many months out of the year is the campus in Rhinebeck open?

Camp is opened ten months out of the year and during the school year we also run some retreats with kids and adults that focus on team building, building self confidence, and communing with the outdoors. We have tremendous interpretive trails and the camp has 40 acres which really gives us a great opportunity to utilize outdoor activities and experiences.

We also have the largest high ropes and low ropes in the metropolitan area because we very much believe that these activities are a common thread that all of these kids can really excel in—it doesn't require them to be academic, it doesn't require them to be competitive; it's a great opportunity for us to build relationships whether its [high ropes or low ropes] or canoeing, hiking, camping in the woods. The different skills within those activities are all framed around building relationships, helping and being helped by another human. So, I'm pretty busy.

(continues on next page)

INTERVIEW

One Perspective on What It Takes
to Make It (continued)

How important is your board of directors to fulfilling the mission of Ramapo for Children?
We have a very active board of directors that is constantly looking at what we are doing and trying to make it better. We are incredibly lucky. I've been here 24 years and there are 10 or 12 board members who have been with me all the way, including one who has been on the board for nearly 60 years. There are 33 board members total and 20 are former camp counselors. One of the reasons to include former counselors to serve on board is because they have a pretty good sense of what it is we do, and what we do well, and their commitment is tested and real and their enthusiasm is unbelievably strong.

How do you know if you have a good board?
Well, number one, they come to meetings, they are interested—they want to be of help, they want to be of service, and they don't see themselves solely in a fiduciary role. You want a board that also sees itself as fulfilling the mission, increasing the quality of service, striving to get the best out of people, and get the best out of themselves.

How many full time staff (excluding summer counselors) do you employ?
We have a full time staff of 42 and a part time staff of around 15. And then we have a contract staff of about 20. The contracted staff—former school superintendents, principals, and teachers—work within the schools to do trainings, workshops and coaching. A lot of our work is ongoing coaching with schools and with the youth service agencies. Altogether with contract, part and full time workers, we are about 75 staff on a year round basis.

What types of people do you look for when you interview potential staff for year round and summer jobs?
We are looking for people who are bright and enthusiastic and eager, willing to work hard, willing to make mistakes, and willing to grow. It takes a number of years before you really catch on, before can really test yourself, before you really can know you should be in a given

field. In my estimate it takes about five years to really figure out if you can be able to say, "I tried that job, I learned that job, I practiced that job, I became a good practitioner." It takes time.

We need people who are willing to make a commitment of time to us. They hope to spend some years with us; they are not just looking to pass through; they are looking to make this their career. Even if they are just making it their career for five to six years, they have a commitment to this field, to their career.

Charity Navigator, a Web site that rates nonprofits based on organizational efficiency and capacity, has given Ramapo for Children its highest rating. Why do you think your nonprofit has been so successful?
We have a strong board, a board that has a clear sense of purpose and mission, a willingness to bring in leadership staff that not just work hard, but have a true commitment to the field at large, meaning this is a field that they want to be in, a field that they love to promote. We have a tremendous campus in which we have invested greatly that is a magnet for people's interest—be it campus interest, retreats, summer camps, training programs. We have a willingness to share our knowledge, to export our knowledge so that our programs are useful not just in a residential setting, but as a great asset within schools and community-based organizations. Pretty much that, and again the longevity is because we have ensured that the leadership staff have opportunities to learn and grow, that they get recognized for their learning, growth, and confidence, and then they get rewarded. You put that all together, and I think you got a chance.

If you could offer words of wisdom to someone just starting out in nonprofit work, what would they be?
Go into your job with a great attitude, showing that you want to learn, you want to grow, you want to test yourself, and you want to see that this is the field that you would like to invest in. Give it your best, be willing to fail and then get up and brush yourself off and get back in there. Work hard and expect others to work hard and give it their best as well. And be willing to cooperate with other people, offer lots of suggestions and interpretations and feedback, so that you are an active participant in the community. Then stay for a little while to ensure that this is a field that you are really interested in, as opposed to just a field that you are passing through, because it takes a while to be good at it. Then once you are good at it, you can share your wealth of experience and your wealth of knowledge. You don't have to stay at it your whole life, but you have to give it enough time that your contribution is a real benefit.

A final aspect regarding dress is to make sure that your workplace knows if you have a religious or cultural reason for wearing certain clothing, head attire, or other accessories. If you have not already presented this information, or if you are hesitant to wear certain clothing even though you would feel more comfortable in it, diplomatically address the matter to find out what is and is not acceptable. Also keep in mind that laws may protect your right to dress according to your religious faith.

Chapter 5

Talk Like a Pro

Trying to understand key nonprofit concepts, as well as the day to day terminology used around the water cooler, can be overwhelming to say the least. This is especially true when nonprofit managers talk about the financial status or the organizational development of a nonprofit. While over time it is certainly possible to pick up the lingo and to understand some of the concepts that are discussed during meetings, in status reports, and in individual evaluations, this chapter will help you to get a head start in learning the language common to nonprofit institutions.

advocacy Advocacy takes place when a person or group appeals to another group, often public officials, in order to further an issue or cause. It is a form of civic action that attempts to get those in power and in the general public to address a concern—whether environmental, social, economic, or medical—that is central to a nonprofit's mission. A nonprofit might advocate on behalf of a group, such as children, that do not have a voice for themselves. Nonprofit advocacy is done by many kinds of nonprofits, although not all. Some nonprofits are categorized as advocacy groups and often engage in lobbying efforts around specific legislation, but advocacy is not lobbying in the legal sense of the term (see definition below).

affinity cards In your wallet you might have a credit card with a logo of your university on it that you got while in school or through your alumnae association. This is an example of cause marketing and it means that your nonprofit school made a deal with a credit card company to partner for a mutual benefit: By using this credit card, a percentage of sales—often one half or 1 percent—is donated to the college and in exchange the credit card company gets access to student and alumnae contact information. Affinity cards often make people feel good because when they use their cards they are supporting a cause they believe in. On the other hand, the cardholder does not get a tax deduction when he or she makes this contribution to the nonprofit—whether a university or a social service agency.

articles of incorporation   A nonprofit is incorporated by its founders in order to create a separate legal entity. This means the nonprofit can own property and a bank account. Submitting these articles also guarantees that the nonprofit will continue on even if the founders are no longer involved. Finally, it protects the nonprofit's founders from personal liability from the nonprofit's operation. The articles of incorporation (sometimes referred to as a *charter*) must be filed with a state office (the appropriate office varies from state to state).

bequest   These involve the transfer of wealth (through a will or a trust) when someone dies that will benefit a charitable organization—a nonprofit or church, for example. Sometimes bequests are done while the donor is still alive. A bequest can involve cash, securities, property, or a percentage of someone's overall estate. Bequests are a form of planned giving and many larger nonprofits have staff that work exclusively with planned giving fund-raising.

best practices   The practices, methods, techniques, attitudes, and other approaches that an organization believes will help it to most effectively and efficiently achieve an outcome. Usually best practices are based on the methods and practices that the nonprofit or similar organizations have used over time that work. These practices are used in many business and nonprofit environments by management, and technical and policy staff.

board of directors   Nonprofits that are registered with the state and federal governments (that is, they are incorporated) will have a volunteer board of directors that oversees the overall conduct of the nonprofit organization—creating guidelines and policies that contribute to its financial health, its programs, and its staff effectiveness. The board is usually responsible for hiring and working with senior staff, monitoring and approving financial decisions and plans, and assessing its own conduct. A nonprofit's charter documents spell out the exact responsibilities of its board, including how long a board member can serve. The board operates as a group and must always work collectively in the nonprofit's best interest, but that does not mean that there is not sometimes tension between the staff and the board. This happens especially when a nonprofit's employees feel that the board is more bottom-line-driven than mission-driven, or when the board feels that the staff does not adequately understand the importance of maintaining a healthy bottom line in order to maintain or grow the nonprofits' programs.

Importantly, some boards are fund-raising boards, and it is expected that if you serve that you will bring in dollars— through business or community contacts and clout—for the nonprofit. Some fund-raising board members are also expected to make personal contributions. Other nonprofits create boards that are expressly not expected to fundraise, sometimes allowing for a more diverse group to become members (including current and former clients of a nonprofit). These are less common than fund-raising boards.

board of trustees Some nonprofits use the term *trustees* instead of directors, but a board of trustees is the same thing as a board of directors. In rare instances a nonprofit will set up a separate board of trustees and board of directors with different bylaws that clearly define their roles.

branding What comes to mind when you think of the American Red Cross or Goodwill Industries? Do you see the logo associated with these well-known nonprofits, or get a mental picture of the Red Cross office in your hometown? Perhaps you see a disaster that the American Red Cross helped to address recently or the trucks full of furniture rolling down busy roads with Goodwill Industries painted on the side. Many images likely come up because these are two nonprofits whose branding has been quite successful. A nonprofit is well-branded when the general public has a host of positive associations that come up when they think about it. Just like for for-profit companies, nonprofits work to brand themselves in order to have the visibility to be successful. Unlike for-profits, the objective of branding is not to sell a product as much as to convince the public to value the nonprofit mission.

bylaws   These are the ruling documents of a nonprofit, and
they delineate how a nonprofit must conduct its business,
including how the board will operate and hire staff. Bylaws
are legal documents and they provide the basic structure and
responsibilities of the board.

capacity building   What is the capacity of a nonprofit to have
a positive impact on its target community? What are the
steps that can be taken actions that will improve nonprofit
effectiveness? These are the questions that both private donors
and the federal government want to better understand, more so
today than ever. Funders of all kinds and the nonprofits they
serve are both looking at the nonprofits' central programs and
projects to determine how to get more return on both money
and time. Efforts geared toward capacity building might include
getting a grant for a nonprofit development fund, providing
training sessions to more productive staff, providing coaching,
and encouraging greater collaboration with other nonprofits.

capital campaign   A large-scale fund-raising campaign initiated
by a nonprofit to fund a specific project such as the construction
or renovation of a university building or the purchase of
expensive technology equipment. Capital campaigns are
sometimes used to make up for money shortfalls because of the
economy, and capital campaigns in down economic times might
refocus their fund-raising to make up for a loss of state funds in
needs-based scholarships, for example.

case statements   Nonprofit fund-raising campaigns all have case
statements, or a statement that provides information to potential
donors about why the organization needs money, what the
funds will be used for, and what how the donor will benefit
by giving to this cause. A case statement is at the center of the
fund-raising plan for all kinds of fund-raisers, including capital,
endowment, and major gifts campaigns.

cause inflation   The growing numbers of nonprofits around
the country sometimes make it difficult for organizations
to distinguish themselves. Cause inflation occurs when a
particular nonprofit cannot distinguish itself and risks not being
able to get the support it needs.

cause marketing   A nonprofit–for-profit partnership first initiated
by American Express in the 1980s. Senior vice president of
American Express Jerry Walsh believed that their credit card users
would be compelled to use their cards more if they could support

causes while doing so (see *affinity cards*). Since the eighties, cause marketing has grown to include a wide range of partnerships, including company product sales where a percentage goes to a nonprofit. Whereas before for-profits were often anonymous philanthropic donors, today they are more likely to look for partnerships that further their own brand while "doing good."

charity   Nonprofit organizations that fall under the 501 (c) (3) tax bracket. Over 50 percent of all nonprofits fall into this category and include arts, education, health care, and human service organizations. Most churches are also considered charities but do not have to register with the Internal Revenue Service. The word *charity* is sometimes used interchangeably with *nonprofit*, but not all nonprofits are charities. Fraternal organizations are nonprofits, but they fall under a different 501 tax status. Veterans groups and orders like the Masons, as well as unions are nonprofits membership groups but they are not charities.

On the Cutting
Edge

Grassroots or Astroturf?

Remember the old ad campaign that asks, "Is it real or is it Memorex?" Well, a similar question has been coming up in recent years around the authenticity of some grass-roots movements: is your movement really grassroots—organized from the ground up—or is it *astroturf*, a movement that looks like a spontaneous response to an issue but is in fact largely orchestrated by corporate or other powerful (often political) interests? In the town hall meetings that took place in the summer of 2009, did the anger and fear really swell from the bottom up around health care reform? How does one distinguish between a true bottom up response to an issue and one that has been highly orchestrated—through money and media campaigns and toolkits—by people in positions of power who have something to gain or lose? In this age of instantaneous dissemination of information through the Internet, both conservatives and liberals and everyone in between will continue to ask these questions and call out those movements that have clear linkages to groups with power.

core values　For a nonprofit, the core values are the values that guide the conduct and action of the staff and volunteers. They reflect how the organization as a whole wants the staff to operate as individuals and collectively. When the core values are understood by the nonprofit staff, they are more able to work toward goals. Core values often include service, integrity, quality, diversity, and shared purpose. In some nonprofits, employees are evaluated at least in part on how well they demonstrate the organization's core values.

corporate foundation　A private foundation sponsored by a for-profit business that makes grants to nonprofits. It is often closely associated with the for-profit that sponsors it, but it is a separate legal entity that follows the same regulations as other private foundations.

corporate philanthropy/giving　When a for-profit corporation donates cash, services such as employee volunteer time, or facilities such as meeting rooms to nonprofit organizations. Sometimes this donation is handled directly by the corporation and sometimes by a private corporate foundation.

direct mail fund-raising　Raising funds for a nonprofit by sending literature through the mail to a membership base or interested stakeholders identified by the nonprofit. Many in the industry believe direct mail is a very good way to increase visibility and the donor base; others do not use direct mail as a central form of fund-raising because it can be quite expensive. To be successful, nonprofits need to understand how to target the right people, craft a strong letter, and provide an easy response mechanism. The quality of a direct mail fund-raising campaign will have a strong impact on its success.

eleemosynary　Dating back to 1616, this term means "that which is related to a charity, or supported by a charity," or it could refer to the organization itself. An eleemosynary educational association is one that is supported by a charity. The word origin relates to the Latin word *eleemosyna,* which means "alms."

endowment　A fund made up of gifts and bequests established by a nonprofit that is invested in order to create an income source for the nonprofit. Often the principal is set aside for the long-term support of an organization, and withdrawals from this principal are based on an amount agreed to by the nonprofit in a spending policy (spendable return), which is determined by the nonprofit board. In hard economic times the endowment will often suffer because investments are subject to the whims of the marketplace. Building endowments allows a nonprofit to engage in long-range planning because an endowment provides a reliable long-term funding stream.

evidence-based practice (EBP)   A term used by social workers and those in various medical fields that means using the best evidence available in order to make good decisions in the care of individual clients and patients. It can also entail spending time with clients in order to consider the clients' views on treatment (sometimes impacted by cultural and other differences) and to respect a client's autonomy. A triangle with corners representing current best evidence, clinical expertise, and client/patient values is often presented to visualize EBT. Since a large percentage of nonprofits are in the area of health and human services, those nonprofits doing direct client work are likely to use EBP.

fiscal year   A fiscal year is the 12 month period in which a nonprofit will use its funds—in other words, its accounting period. All financial transactions for that year are compiled together, added up, and reported on. For many nonprofits, the fiscal year ends on July 31st.

foundation   An institution supported by an endowment or other permanent funds. A private foundation is supported by funds from a small number of people, such as the Bill and Linda Gates and Carnegie Foundations. A public foundation is supported by many donors—both organizations and individuals. Both public and private foundations are nonprofits that usually invest in a specific cause or set of causes by granting money to nonprofits that (usually) compete for these funds. A community foundation is supported by several donors for the long-term benefit of the people in one defined geographic area. They are smaller foundations that provide services to donors who wish to establish endowed funds without the costs of starting independent foundations. There are also independent federal agencies that are government foundations—created by Congress (mostly in the 1950s and 1960s) to promote specific areas of interest. The National Science Foundation and the National Endowment for the Arts are two examples, and both of them provide substantial funds to thousands on nonprofit organizations all over the United States.

founder's syndrome　Some nonprofit founders and leaders in a nonprofit are a force to be reckoned with. When that force is too great, however—when the personality of a leader in the organization eclipses the organization's mission—you are dealing with founder's syndrome. In concrete terms, a nonprofit with founder's syndrome has a leader that feels he or she has to be involved in every decision the organization makes, often making decisions without input from other staff, and that tends to react to crises rather than implement strategies with others to prevent problems. Founder's syndrome usually involves a CEO that feels like the board works for him or her, not for the nonprofit mission.

Google grants　Did you know that your nonprofit might be able to get some free advertising from a prominent company that is literally all over the Internet? According to Google's Web site, "Google Grants is a unique in-kind donation program awarding free AdWords advertising to select charitable organizations. We support organizations sharing our philosophy of community service to help the world in areas such as science and technology, education, global public health, the environment, youth advocacy, and the arts."

grant　A subsidy or gift given to a nonprofit (by a foundation, individual donor, or other institution). Grants are often subject to certain conditions by the grantor. The potential grantee must often compete with other nonprofits by writing a grant proposal that provides information detailing why the nonprofit organization or one of its programs merits the grant.

grassroots campaign　A campaign that is initiated and organized by ordinary people, often with the assistance of nonprofit staff and volunteers, to get out information and generate actions around an issue or concern. It is a bottom-up approach to organizing groups of people, not top-down (directed by people in positions of economic and political power), and nonprofit employees often have been trained in strategies for building grassroots support for a cause. Nonprofits also might hire canvassers and organizers to get the message out around an issue—affordable health care, labor rights, gun owners rights—in order to help create a grassroots campaign at local, state, or national levels.

green jobs　Jobs with an environmental focus. A green job might involve installing solar panels, increasing energy efficiency, or leading a conservation project. Over the next several years, there is expected to be a surge in federal and private spending for jobs that are related to protecting and conserving our natural resources.

greenwashing When a company or other entity promotes its programs or products which are not in environmentally friendly in any meaningful way as "green" in order to cash in on the "green" trend.

incorporation Just like for-profits, a nonprofit organization must be incorporated—it must submit information to a state agency in order to be recognized as a corporation. For nonprofits, this is one of the first steps it must complete in order for it to be considered for IRS tax-exempt status. It involves several steps, including choosing a name for the organization, filing articles of incorporation, submitting bylaws, applying for federal and state tax exemption, and appointing a board of directors.

incubator A nonprofit incubator (like a business incubator) provides funding, technical resources, management training, and other comprehensive services to new and early stage nonprofits. Sometimes the designated incubator co-locates nonprofits together in order to share facilities and expertise.

Fast
Facts

Surprisingly So

Some interesting and perhaps surprising nonprofit organizations:

- The National Rifle Association
- 4-H Foundation
- The National Football League
- The National Geographic
- MS Magazine
- Chambers of Commerce
- The College Board (the group that responsible for the Scholastic Aptitude Test, or SAT, and other testing materials)

independent sector A term that covers all charitable, social welfare, and church-related nonprofits. All nonprofits and religious congregations are part of the independent sector. The entities excluded from this sector are commercial for-profits and government agencies.

in-kind donation/contribution When someone gives a service, product, or item to a nonprofit, *not* a cash donation. In-kind donations given to a 501(c) (3) nonprofit organization, especially donations of goods such as food or clothing, are sometimes tax-deductible based on the fair market value of the donation. When nonprofits solicit funds for their agency or a program, they usually also make a call for in-kind donations, knowing that there are many groups—schools, churches, companies—that would like to be a part of service projects or fund-raisers for a cause.

input What an organization invests in their programs in terms of physical, financial, and human resources.

Internal Revenue Service (IRS) Form 990 Every nonprofit that has annual receipts of $1 million or more, or total assets of $2.5 million or more must fill out a 990 form with the IRS. This form provides essential information about a nonprofit—its mission, finances, governance, operations, and programs— and is available to government regulators, the press, and the public. A 990 form is a good way for a job seeker to get vital information about the nonprofits they might target in their job search or before they go in for an interview. There are also free Web sites, such as Guidestar.org, where anyone can access form 990 information on over a million nonprofit organizations.

knowledge workers A term coined by management expert Peter Drucker in the late fifties to describe a new class of nonacademic intellectuals. These workers are valued because of their expertise in a field and through their understanding of the field based on interpretation and analysis. In later years Drucker applied this term to the growing nonprofit sector, detailing how for-profits can learn from nonprofits and vice-versa, as well as how knowledge workers can find meaningful work in nonprofit management.

lobbying The IRS defines lobbying as "direct and grassroots action to promote specific legislation at the local, state, and national levels of government." The IRS, while allowing nonprofit lobbying, limits the amount a nonprofit can spend, and the amount differs depending on whether it falls under direct or grassroots lobbying. Direct lobbying is defined as "as an attempt to influence legislation by stating a position on specific legislation to legislators or other government employees who participate in the formulation of legislation, or urging your members to do so." Grassroots lobbying also involves influencing legislation by promoting a position, but the influence is directed toward the general public. Not all nonprofits lobby, but many do, including the Children's Defense Fund, the Humane Society, and Focus on the Family.

logic model   A model used by program managers and other nonprofit managers to describe and assess the effectiveness of their programs. It provides the logical linkages among the various parts of a program. Once it has been described, performance outcomes can be evaluated. A logic model is usually depicted with a graph that includes inputs (what an organization invests in terms of physical, monetary and human resources), outputs (program activities such as workshops and publications that have been produced), and short-, medium-, and long-term outcomes (changes in knowledge, behaviors, or economic situation).

matching gift   When an employer matches someone's donation with a donation of an equal or greater amount to a nonprofit organization. A company or individual might agree to match the amount donated in a period of time to an on-air fund-raiser: If listeners call in to pledge $10,000 during a two-hour period, a company will match the collective gift, bringing to total to $20,000. Matching gifts allow individuals and groups to double the impact of a donation.

mission   Every nonprofit has a mission. The best ones are succinct, yet powerful. The mission is the statement about a nonprofit that includes who the agency is, what type of organization it is, what it does, who it serves, and where it operates. For example, the American Cancer Society has the following mission for its U.S. programs: "The American Cancer Society is the nationwide, community-based, voluntary health organization dedicated to eliminating cancer as a major health problem by preventing cancer, saving lives, and diminishing suffering from cancer, through research, education, advocacy, and service." Some missions can be quite powerful even if they do not provide detailed information, such as the YMCA's mission "To put Christian Principles into practice through programs that build Spirit, Mind and Body for all." If a nonprofit is relatively young or is not national or international in scope, it is important that the mission include the values of the organization, the geographic reach of its services or programs, and the purpose of the organization.

Model Nonprofit Corporation Act   A group of rulings by the American Bar Association that can be adopted by states to regulate nonprofits in their jurisdictions. The act includes "requirements that a state can use for registration of nonprofits and what also needs to be included in articles of incorporation and the bylaws in order for the IRS to accept the nonprofit as tax-exempt. Nonprofit-operating structure, the voting process, mergers and the sale of assets are also covered." It is not mandatory that a state adopt the regulations, but it can adopt some or all of them.

National Volunteer Week   A week in April set aside, according to the Points of Light Foundation, to "celebrate the ordinary people who accomplish extraordinary things through service." This week started in 1974 as an annual celebration of volunteerism, and every president since Richard Nixon has signed a proclamation promoting the week. In recent times it has been sponsored by the nonprofit Points of Light Foundation and Volunteer Center National Network and includes events recognizing outstanding individuals across the country. The Points of Light Foundation (Pointsoflight.org) provides a free downloadable toolkit with extensive Volunteer Week information, a timeline for submitting names of volunteers for competitive and noncompetitive volunteer awards, as well as sample templates and forms that nonprofits and other organizations can use to promote National Volunteer Week.

nongovernmental organization (NGO)   These organizations— also called international nongovernmental organizations, or INGOs—use private and public funding to support work in developing countries. They appeared first between the first and second world wars to provide relief to European war victims. Their numbers continued to increase after World War II, in large part because of the end of European colonialism and the emergence of newly independent countries. Economic development assistance and awareness of international poverty have spurred the growth of NGOs. Since the 1980s, NGOs have played a huge role in helping to fill the gaps in assistance caused by government fiscal crises or privatization that limits resources to the poor and underserved around the globe. Many NGOs have headquarters or offices in the United States. This is a growing area of employment for people with backgrounds in nonprofit work.

nonprofit organization (NPO)   A nonprofit is formed by a group that unites around a specific cause or purpose. While most nonprofits are tax exempt under the IRS 501 tax codes, not all nonprofits file for tax exempt status (see *unincorporated nonprofit association*). Moreover, nonprofits can and often do make a profit off of a good or service, but the nonprofit must reinvest the profit in the organization or use it for charitable purposes in their target community. Nonprofits do not have shareholders, as public for-profit companies do, and are guided by values rather than by financial commitments. Charities are nonprofits, as are many professional associations, labor unions, churches, performing arts centers, and research institutes.

operating expenses   Those expenses that are part of the day-to-day administrative operations of a nonprofit organization, including staff payroll, employee benefits, and transportation costs.

organized abandonment   A term coined by management authority Peter Drucker used to describe the need to evaluate the programs in a company or nonprofit that are not producing, and therefore that should not be continued. Drucker advised both for-profits and nonprofits, but the application to nonprofits was novel because he insisted that, like in for-profits, certain programs should be killed if the organization was trying to be too many things to too many people. Unlike for-profits however, a program should not be killed just because it is not paying for itself. If a service is critically needed in a community, and the nonprofit is the only one providing it or providing it better than others, it has an obligation not to abandon that program. However, if a nonprofit is spreading itself too thinly, then it needs to abandon programs that are not working or that suck too much time, money, and human resources from other programs. In recent years Drucker's idea has been implemented by nonprofits by using an organized abandonment grid, a tool for evaluating the

Best
Practice

Drucker's Advice

Peter F. Drucker (1909–2005) was a veritable fount of best practice information for both nonprofit and for-profit managers. Known as the "father of management," he focused some of his attention later in life on nonprofit management. In his book *Managing the Nonprofit Organization*, he provides the following best practices and words of wisdom for nonprofit leaders:

- "In every move, in every decision, in every policy, the non-profit institution needs to start out by asking, Will this advance our capacity to carry out our mission? It should start with the end result, should focus outside-in rather than inside-out."

- "Good causes do not excuse bad manners. Bad manners rub people raw; they do leave permanent scars. And good manners make a difference."

- "Include everyone in the organization in your efforts to build the organization around communication, not around a set hierarchy. Everyone must know how to get the right information by asking the right questions: What information do I need to do *my* job—from whom, when, how? And: What information do I owe others so that they can do *their* job, in what form, and when?"

- For senior staff: "Force your people, and especially your executives, to be on the outside often enough to know what the institution exists for...Effective nonprofits make sure that their people get out into the field and actually work there again and again."

social purpose and the financial impact of all of a nonprofit's programs and then weighing them against each other.

outcomes/outcomes chain What does the nonprofit staff want their organization or separate programs to accomplish? That is the outcome, and includes such goals as expanding service delivery or improved coordination in service. An outcome is often written down as a straightforward outcome statement, which includes the type of change, applied to whom, in what way, and for which programs. An outcomes chain is how the nonprofit or nonprofit program sequences the outcomes since they cannot all happen at once and sometimes depend on each other. The outcomes chains also demarcate the progression of outcomes into short-term, intermediate, and long-term outcomes.

outcomes based evaluation (OBE)   An evaluation tool used by nonprofits—especially social services nonprofits—to assess their impact on clients. While OBE is also used in other sectors, an OBE analysis tool was developed by the United Way in 1995 in order for nonprofits to streamline their reporting to the federal government when using federal funds in their programs. This approach looks at the effects and advantages that clients experience during and after they have participated in a nonprofit agency's program. In other words, this tool helps a nonprofit (and often its funders) to better understand whether the nonprofit has truly made a difference in its target group's lives, and if so, how exactly it made a difference. It also provides nonprofits with a way to demonstrate public accountability in the use of their funds to funders, stakeholders, and the community at large.

output   Output measures what nonprofit organizations do based on the production of the service activities in which they are engaged. In other words, an output is what is produced (a good or service) in a stated time period.

philanthropic giving index (PGI)   This index gauges nonprofit fund-raisers' confidence in the current climate for fund-raising. It was created in 1997 by Indiana University's Center on Philanthropy after researchers completed a study of the climate for philanthropic gifts and fund-raising in the United States. The PGI "measures the climate for philanthropic giving in much the same way that the Consumer Confidence Index assesses the environment for consumer purchases. The PGI focuses on current and expected donor behavior." The PGI is made up of two separate parts: The Present Situation Index and the Expectations Index. The former surveys nonprofit fund-raisers to assess the current giving environment and the latter determines the climate for the next six months. The overall PGI is an average of the two indexes.

philanthropy   Efforts that are voluntary and organized to promote a social good. Philanthropy means the giving of charitable aid or donations as part of that effort.

pledges   A written or verbal promise to make a contribution at a later date. Nonprofits will often place "pledges/grants receivable" on their balance sheet in order to show the amount of money it can plausibly expect to receive in the future.

positioning statement   One or two sentences that a nonprofit employee will use (usually developed by the nonprofit managers and marketing) to reply to someone who asks what the organization does.

request for proposal (RFP)   This is an invitation from a funding entity (for-profit company, foundation, or government agency) to submit an application for funding for a particular cause. It is a way for some foundations to promote a new program and it is becoming more common in nonprofit funding circles. The following RFP announcement is typical: "Verizon Wireless and The Verizon Foundation announced today a request for proposals (RFP) inviting nonprofits in Maine, New Hampshire and Vermont to apply for a total of $100,000 in grants to support domestic violence prevention and service programs... Through the 2009 Verizon Foundation Domestic Violence Solutions Awards RFP, nonprofit agencies in northern New England are invited to compete for grants of up to $10,000 to support domestic violence service initiatives."

restricted and unrestricted funds   Restricted funds are those provided by donors who have limited their donation to one kind of program or purpose, such as student scholarships. Unrestricted funds are donations that can be used for any expenses, including operating expenses.

return on investment (ROI)   An evaluation tool that helps a nonprofit determine the benefits, the costs, and the value of a technology over time. It can be used before a technology purchase to help determine if a particular investment is a good idea, or it might be used to analyze a technology pilot project that the nonprofit is considering expanding. How does the technology advance the program or improve a service? Does this technology (or will it) increase the efficiency of the staff? These and many other questions go into a ROI analysis.

Sarbanes-Oxley Act of 2002   Passed after the accounting scandals of Enron and others in 2001 and 2002, this law requires publicly-traded companies to adopt new governing standards that will increase the board members' role in overseeing the finances and the auditing procedures of for-profit companies. If these standards are lacking, the government can step in and take over regulation of the company's finances. One provision that applies to both nonprofits and for-profits closes most of the loopholes with respect to document destruction and whistle-blower protection. Most provisions beyond the aforementioned do not yet apply to nonprofits, but many in the nonprofit community believe that they soon might.

service learning   A strategy that incorporates meaningful community service (often through a nonprofit organization) into traditional education. It is a way of teaching students in schools, in churches, and through community organizations in a way that enriches and transforms their relationship to the cause as well as provides a much needed service to a community.

social entrepreneur   A person in the nonprofit sector that combines his or her passion for a social cause with a business-like approach—including discipline, accountability, and fiscal responsibility. A social entrepreneur is also defined as a wealthy person that wants to use their money to fundamentally impact an issue (local, national, or international in scope). In the United States, Al Gore and Robert Redford would be considered social entrepreneurs for their financial and social commitment to environmental issues. The goal of the social entrepreneur is to go beyond an immediate problem to fundamentally change communities, countries, regions, and, the hope may be, the whole world.

social media   All media that involves social interaction, which is now most prevalent on the Internet. Blogs, sites like Facebook, Twitter, MySpace, Youtube, and LinkedIn (for business networking) are examples of social media. For nonprofits, using social media has become a way to connect people and groups with similar interests. Some nonprofits use different forms to generate interest in their cause: Through a savvy understanding of social media, nonprofits are able to fundraise, increase membership, break news, generate buzz with a video or podcast, or promote an event or campaign at local, regional, national, or international levels.

sponsorship   A nonprofit asks a company or corporation to sponsor a fund-raising event with a donation of money. Companies like to provide visible logos when they give money to a fund-raiser in order to tie their brand to the nonprofit. They also prefer to sponsor nonprofits that bring in a large number of people, especially people that might be interested in their brand. For example, if the local Humane Society asks a dog food company to sponsor a community fund-raiser, they will be enticed to say yes when they learn that a thousand dog owners or more will be there. Nonprofits often offer sponsorship opportunities at different levels. For example, by donating $50 the company gets a small ad in the fund-raising program flyer; for $1,000 the company gets a large sponsor banner at the fund-raising event, the company name is announced during an event speech, or a dinner table has a visible plaque that indicates the event is supported by the sponsor.

stakeholder   For nonprofits, a stakeholder is anyone who has or might have an interest, or stake, in the organization, including donors, volunteers, members, clients, the board of directors, companies that work with the nonprofit, and employees. To be a successful nonprofit is to make sure that the stakeholders are satisfied.

stewardship   In a nonprofit, stewardship usually refers to taking good care of an organization's donors and other stakeholders. This is done when nonprofit managers assure donors and stakeholders that they will properly make use of and develop the organization's resources, including its people, its property, and its financial assets. Stewardship in difficult economic times includes continuing to cultivate donors by staying in touch and letting them know that they are valued. Recognizing a donor's contribution through consistent stewardship helps to nurture future giving to the nonprofit.

SWOT analysis   SWOT stands for **s**trengths, **w**eaknesses, **o**pportunities, and **t**hreats and often is part of a nonprofit's strategic planning. Strengths include the internal factors that have helped a nonprofit to be successful such as a steady cash flow; weaknesses are those internal factors that can weaken a nonprofit such as high staff turnover; opportunities are the external factors that might help your nonprofit, such as a strong economy; and threats are the external factors that might have a negative impact, such as a new competing nonprofit or a poor economy. A SWOT analysis is most accurate when every level of the nonprofit staff is involved in strategic planning, and it can help a nonprofit identify branding opportunities.

tag line   A short, powerful statement that sums up what a nonprofit organization does and why it is valuable. This statement

Fast Facts

The Future of Social Media

Social media has its advocates but also its doubters. Nonprofits need to be well-versed in choosing the best platforms before throwing time and money into social media marketing. Some nonprofits, in their attempts to explore social media, are finding that just because someone joins your Facebook page or becomes a "fan" does not mean that they will become active in or donate money to your cause. Nonprofits sites and bloggers have noted that, in fact, old fashioned direct mail campaigns still outperform Internet fund-raising for most organizations.

So how do nonprofits reach the millions of social media users, and especially the so-called millennials or generation Y—young adults born since 1980? To reach this technologically savvy group, nonprofits need to understand how this generation is utilizing social media. For example, unlike older Americans, younger adults often eschew traditional media, are reluctant to fill out membership forms, and are less loyal to brands. However, when loyal they will file-share and pass along clips and blogs to a wide network of online friends. Time will tell whether social media will be a better source for fund-raising, publicity, and membership growth than traditional forms. But it will not just happen because a nonprofit throws up a Facebook page or starts a Twitter account.

should be linked to the nonprofit's positioning statement, and a memorable nonprofit tag line will make a reader (or listener) perk up and take notice, perhaps for the first time. For example, the tagline for the American Lung Association is "Improving life, one breathe at a time." UNICEF's tagline "Whatever it takes to save a child," suggests a committed and compassionate organization. Taglines help a nonprofit to brand or rebrand itself.

tax exempt status Most nonprofits are tax exempt under their 501 (c) status, meaning they do not have to pay the same taxes—such as property tax and income tax (depending on state as well as federal guidelines)—as a for-profit company. Charitable nonprofits that file will receive exemption under

501 (c) (3) of the tax code. Civic leagues or groups file under
501 (c) (4) status. Acquiring 501 (c) statuses is done by
filing an application with the IRS. There are 27 kinds of 501
(c) organizations that are tax-exempt, including cemetery
companies, social and recreation clubs, and Veterans'
organizations. Additionally, most churches are tax exempt,
though not required by law to fill out IRS forms.

third sector   Another word describing the nonprofit sector of the
economy—organizations that are not part of the government
and not part of the for-profit marketplace.

underwriting   Underwriting is when a for-profit company or a
foundation sponsors a service, such as a public radio program.
In exchange, the for-profit organization is mentioned during the
programming. The Federal Communications Commission limits
the content of underwriting announcements on public radio in
order to protect the non-commercial content that the listeners of
public radio value and expect. Companies cannot, for example,
discuss pricing information or enticements to buy something.

unincorporated nonprofit association   A nonprofit group
that has decided not to incorporate, which means that they are
not tax-exempt and usually do not have the legal protections
of corporations (this differs from state to state). This kind
of association only requires two or more members to come
together for a common nonprofit function.

Volunteer Protection Act   An act passed in 1997 that protects
nonprofit volunteers from having a claim filed against them if
the nonprofit carries an adequate amount of liability insurance.
There are limits to the protection—the law protects the
volunteer against claims of negligence but not against claims of
gross negligence, for instance—and therefore it is incumbent
upon the nonprofit to understand exactly how its volunteers are
protected.

workplace giving program   A program under which an
employee signs up to give a percentage of their paycheck or a
fixed dollar amount to a nonprofit group of their choice—or
of their company's choice. Perhaps the best-known workplace
giving program is the United Way, which generates millions
of dollars through their annual workplace giving campaigns.
While the United Way is a national nonprofit, the money
generated by different United Ways city chapters around the
United States will be spent on the children, families, and

community programs in the same city or region. Workplace giving programs are employer-sponsored and sometimes a company will provide a matching gift for the selected nonprofit or nonprofits. There is often an option for the employee to write in a nonprofit or choose a cause from a list of nonprofits that is the most near and dear to an employee's heart.

Chapter 6

Resources

The list of resources in this chapter is a starting point for further research and exploration. Many of these resources have Web sites—so take time to look over the ones that best match up with your interests and explore away!

Associations and Organizations

Nonprofit associations and organizations help you to stay in conversation with other professionals in order to network, to understand the latest trends and tools, and even to commiserate when times are challenging or when you are considering transitioning to a different organization or job. The following list of organizations is not exhaustive, but rather it includes national chapters of organizations and associations most closely associated with nonprofits. Keep in mind that many national groups have state or regional associations that hold meetings and conferences, which will help you to be in the know. They also often have Web sites with jobs listings, e-newsletters, and journals specific to a nonprofit subsector.

Alliance for Nonprofit Management is for individuals and organizations interested in capacity building, or improving the management and governance capability of nonprofit organizations. If you are a consultant, if you create training programs or research and write about nonprofits, if you train nonprofit managers, or if you provide technology solutions, this organization says that it is for you. Members include management support organizations, research and academic programs, and publishing groups that provide technical training and consulting to nonprofits. The Alliance also puts out the *Alliance Insights* e-newsletter. (http://www.allianceonline.org)

American Association of Grant Professionals (AAGP) is a membership organization for grant professionals (in government, educational, and nonprofits organizations), whose purpose is to advance grantsmanship as a profession. It publishes a semi-annual journal that focuses on best practices and scholarly research on the profession. One of its main goals is to establish a credentialing process. (http://grantprofessionals.org)

American Grant Writers' Association (AGWA) is a key organization for grant writers of all backgrounds. According to their Web site, "AGWA members are Grant Consultants, employees of State or Local Government Agencies, or employees of Non-Profit Organizations throughout the United States...AGWA offers the Certified Grant Writer(r) Credential to those members who have demonstrated proficiency in grant researching and writing. AGWA also hosts an Annual Conference where members can improve skills, learn new trends, and network." (http://www.agwa.us)

Association of Fundraising Professionals (AFP) is an international membership organization for fund-raisers. The AFP has 30,000 members in 206 chapters throughout the world and provides an online resource center, professional development courses, access to fund-raising resources, and a job center. (http://www.afpnet.org)

Independent Sector is a national association made up of over 600 charities, foundations, and corporate giving programs, as well as students at academic centers working on philanthropic research, individuals, and for-profit companies working with nonprofits. The purpose of this group is to mobilize and strengthen the charitable community "in order to fulfill our vision of a just and inclusive society and a healthy democracy of active citizens, effective institutions, and vibrant communities." This organization holds a national conference and has several committees to help grantors to develop collective strategies. Current committee topics include "protecting advocacy rights of nonprofits, promoting tax incentives for charitable giving, and addressing federal and state budget concerns." The Independent Sector also is concerned with maintaining the highest ethical practices throughout the non-profit sector and often serves as the official voice to media, government, and business groups. (http://www.independentsector.org)

National Alliance of Community Economic Development Associations is an alliance of community economic development (CED) practitioners and their CED organizations. These are groups that work to provide affordable housing, to impact positive economic development, and to obtain essential services for seniors, families, people with disabilities, and the poor and homeless. (http://www.naceda.org)

Everyone Knows

Ask For Help

Make sure that you check with your nonprofit to see if they will help with or provide membership fees for you to join associations or organizations.

National Association of Youth Service Consultants (NAYSC) is a membership-based organization for professional consultants and experts that provides an extensive listing of consulting and funding opportunities, technical assistance providers, nonprofits, and subject-matter experts in several areas common to many human services nonprofits, such as workforce development, juvenile justice, child welfare, mental health, and disabilities. According to their Web site, "NAYSC was formed in 2003 to improve services for youth, by linking expertise to the agencies and organizations in need of technical assistance and consulting services in all youth service areas." (http://www.naysc.org/index.html)

National Committee on Responsive Philanthropy (NCRP) is a nonprofit watchdog group that works to assure that philanthropic organizations serve the public good, respond to communities with the least wealth and opportunity, and maintain the highest of possible standards for openness and honesty. Members include grantors and foundations, as well as advocacy and watchdog groups. Membership benefits include receiving information about making philanthropy more accessible to the disadvantaged, especially through *Responsive Philanthropy*—NCRP's quarterly newsletter—and the e-newsletter called NCRP Roundup. (http://www.ncrp.org/paib)

National Counsel of Nonprofits is, according to its Web site, a "network of state and regional nonprofit associations serving more than 20,000 member organizations." Its purpose is to link local organizations to a national audience through state associations. In this way it can help small and midsize nonprofits understand key management issues, collaborate and network with other nonprofits, understand and participate in policy issues that impact the sector, and have a greater influence within their communities. (http://www.councilofnonprofits.org)

National Human Services Assembly includes national nonprofits in the fields of health, human and community development, and human services. Its primary goal is to "Provide collective leadership to shape national human development/health & human service strategies." (http://www.nassembly.org)

Nonprofit Academic Centers Council (NACC) is a membership association that includes those academic centers or programs at accredited colleges and universities that focus on the study of nonprofit organizations, voluntarism, or philanthropy. (http://www.naccouncil.org/default.asp)

Society for Nonprofit Organizations (SNPO) is a nonprofit management support organization with 6,000 members. The SNPO puts out a bi-monthly magazine, grant and job listings, and has an extensive online archive with articles on boards, fund-raising, taxation, management, public relations, and volunteers. (http://www.snpo.org)

Books and Periodicals

Books and periodicals about nonprofits can inspire and educate. If you have read about the history of nonprofits and want to learn more, if you think it behooves you to stay on top of major nonprofit issues and trends, or if you want advice or inspiration from nonprofit experts in various fields, this list is a good place to start. Some of the most motivating and thought-provoking journals and books are explained in some detail; others are included for you to explore on your own.

Books

Cause Marketing for Nonprofits: Partner for Purpose, Passion, and Profits. By Jocelyne Daw (John Wiley & Sons, 2006). This is a highly readable book, especially for those in nonprofits that are considering venturing into mutually beneficial alliances with for-profits. It includes best practices, non-profit driven branding ideas, the nuts and bolts of how to implement a cause marketing program, and provides specific successful examples of cause marketing done right.

Inventing the Nonprofit Sector. By Peter Dobkin Hall (The John Hopkins University Press, 1992). Peter Dobkin Hall is one of only a handful of U.S. historians who have done extensive research and writing on the history of nonprofits in the United States. This book is perhaps his most comprehensive review of the nonprofit sector. Hall writes that his major aims in this book are to "chronicle the long and complex conversation about the role of nonprofit institutions in American democracy, how the public in this same democracy defines itself, and how scholarship has played a role in these 'dramas of self-definition.'" This book is not exactly a light read, but it is an important one for those who truly want a deeper understanding of the events, people, and institutions that have shaped what we call the nonprofit sector today.

Jossey-Bass Handbook of Nonprofit Leadership and Management. Edited by Robert Herman and Associates (John Wiley & Sons, 2005). The purpose of this book is to explore leadership and management practices in the nonprofit sector. Each chapter is written by a different scholar or practitioner in the nonprofit field. Chapters include "The Internationalization of the Nonprofit Sector," "Nonprofit Lobbying," "Outcome Assessment and Program Evaluation," and "Principles of Training for Volunteers and Employees."

Making the Nonprofit Sector in the United States. By David C. Hammack, Ed. (Indiana University Press, 1998). A good source for readers interested in learning about the primary historical documents that have directly impacted the development and practices of the nonprofit sector. Excerpts from each document is introduced and framed by editor David Hammack. The book is structured chronologically into four sections that deal with central economic, political, and constitutional developments.

Managing the Nonprofit Sector. By Peter F. Drucker (HarperCollins Publishers, 1990). This book by the highly respected management guru is specifically for nonprofit managers. Written two decades ago, Drucker's words of wisdom are still very relevant today. It is also written in an anecdote-filled and conversational voice that is engrossing and thought-provoking. The many interviews with nonprofit leaders around the county provide extremely useful tips that are still germane and that might encourage you to suggest a new project or take a new approach in your job.

Shameless Exploitation: In Pursuit of the Common Good. By Paul Newman and A.E. Hotchner (Nan Talese, 2003). A fun and often humorous read about how Paul Newman and A. E. Hatchner started their food empire, donating all of their profits to charity at the end of every fiscal year and then starting over again. While not everyone has the access to the people and start-up funds that a celebrity like Newman does, the reader will be surprised how difficult initially it was—even with some financial advantages—to get people to take them seriously and to get their products in stores. More importantly, their book details the incredible commitment and energy of Newman in forming his nonprofit camp for terminally ill children and how he was able, against many odds, to get it up and running in a remarkably short period of time. Perhaps the most interesting aspect of the book is the section about other camps that Newman and Hotchner helped nonprofits to start and how and why these camps faced difficulties and obstacles both in the United States and overseas.

Periodicals

Chronicle of Higher Education is similar to the Chronicle of Philanthropy but is focused specifically on U.S. universities and colleges. Much of the content online is free but some topics are available to subscribers for a fee. On this publication's pages, the professor, college administrator, or graduate student embarking on a job search will read about average faculty salaries by field and rank, as well as surveys that provide information on the best places for junior faculty to work. This is the place for new faculty and administrators to go to find jobs in the field, be they administrative, faculty, or executive jobs. (http://chronicle.com/section/Home/5)

Chronicle of Philanthropy is a print and online guide to all things related to nonprofits and a must-read for anyone in nonprofit management. The tag line is "The Newspaper of the Nonprofit World" and that it is, providing articles on the state of the industry, comprehensive job listings, and up-to-date and easy to search conference and nonprofit event information. Do not miss the rich array of podcasts about issues like social media strategies, and be sure to look through information on the companies that are giving even in a difficult economic climate. Finally, this journal will keep you informed on key governmental proposals and how they might impact nonprofits. Most of the chronicle's content is free online, including links to the best nonprofit blogs and other resources that are only a click away. (http://philanthropy.com)

International Journal of Non Profit and Voluntary Sector Marketing is a subscription-only journal (available in print and online form) that "provides an international forum for peer-reviewed papers and case studies on the latest techniques, thinking and best practice in marketing for the not-for-profit sector." (http://www.wiley.com/WileyCDA/WileyTitle/productCd-NVSM.html)

Nonprofit Times is a print and online publication that is a resource for all things related to nonprofit management. A very nice feature of the online version is the ability to get frequent topical updates via e-mail. The Web site and print journal also provide extensive nonprofit job listings, a large resource directory, and frequent guides and reports based on surveys of people in the nonprofit field. For example, every year the journal puts out a *Power & Influence Top 50 Guide*, an unscientific list (based on nonprofit employees' votes) of the top 50 nonprofit leaders around the country that are doing truly interesting and innovative things. This is a great place to increase your understanding of what it might take to make it to the very top, as well as to further explore the biographies, writings, and approaches of the leaders—some well-known outside the sector but many who are not. (http://www.nptimes.com/09sep/toc090901.html)

Philanthropy Matters is the journal of The Center on Philanthropy at Indiana University. You can download this journal in PDF form for free. (http://www.philanthropy.iupui.edu/Research/PhilanthropyMatters)

Philanthropy News Digest is an online daily news service of the Foundation Center, bringing together the best print and online philanthropy-related articles every Tuesday. Also includes a Request For Proposal (RFP) bulletin published every Friday with new funding possibilities for nonprofits, and a job corner with numerous nonprofit job postings. (http://foundationcenter.org/pnd/info/about.jhtml;jsessionid=H01IQGEOFO2AHLAQBQ4CGXD5AAAACI2F)

Keeping
in Touch

Know Your Audience

The number of blogs today is truly impressive, including those about nonprofits. Staying up to date on pertinent nonprofit blogs is a good way to be in touch with the movers and shakers in your area of nonprofit work. This is especially true for fund-raisers who can learn and network with other fund-raisers as well as funders. Make sure that if you do blog that you are careful to know your audience and are very clear about what you are trying to convey in your comments. Your aim is to engage and maybe even to impress. Make sure that your writing skills are up to the task.

Philanthropy Journal is an online journal that provides a daily Web site and weekly e-mail bulletins free of charge. The journal offers timely news round-ups, nonprofit resources, and job listings. (http://www.philanthropyjournal.org/news/top-stories)

Web Sites

To list and describe all of the Web sites dedicated to all things nonprofit is impossible. With that in mind, here is a small list of what is out there for the nonprofit professional.

The Agitator carries the tag line, "Fundraising & Advocacy Strategies, Trends, Tips . . . With an Edge." This site offers up blogs and links to news about fund-raising and advocacy and encourages you to "get agitated" by signing up for its daily e-mails or joining its premium service. This site is a great way to stay up to date on the latest nonprofit trends, as well as to view some comical videos. (http://www.theagitator.net)

Don't Tell the Donor explains itself as, "An anonymous source of news and opinions from the world of nonprofit fund-raising . . . whether it's ripped from the headlines or gossip from development offices... these are the stories you might not want to tell the donor." Although not updated on a regular basis, this site provides some good humor (cartoons, *Onion*-like blogs) and a great list with links to other nonprofit blogs online. (http://donttellthedonor.blogspot .com)

The Idealist is a truly wonderful site initiated by the nonprofit Action Without Borders in 1995 where "people and organizations can exchange resources and ideas, locate opportunities and supporters, and take steps toward building a world where all people can lead free and dignified lives." This site provides a veritable one-stop shopping trip for anyone wanting to learn as much as they can about the nonprofit sector, available jobs, answers to frequently asked questions (FAQs), speakers, people, campaigns, internships—and the list goes on. (http://www.idealist.org)

Nonprofit Matrix is "an online directory of web services, portals, consultants, and software vendors offering essential tools and services to assist nonprofits and charities." (http://www.nonprofitmatrix.com)

501c3Cast is an enjoyable collection of podcasts hosted by a nonprofit professional named Corey Pudhorodsky on a wide array of topics. The site describes 501c3Cast as "an independent podcast produced by a few people who care about helping nonprofit professionals, not-for-profit volunteers, and other 'do-gooders' in the philanthropic world" and Corey begins the podcast with the friendly "Greetings, do-gooders!" Here are some examples of past podcasts: Interview with Bob Grim of The Corporation for National and Community Service about VolunteeringInAmerica.gov; NGO Connection from Microsoft; Nonprofit Tag Lines Awards; and Nonprofit Marketing Report. (http://coreyp501c3.libsyn.com)

New Voices of Philanthropy is a visually-engaging site created by Trista Harris for young and upcoming nonprofit professionals involved in foundation work. Blogs are lively and compelling, and include tips and words of wisdom from philanthropy sages. Blogs entries include, for example, "Holy Crap, That's a Great Idea!"; "Let's Hear More about Work for Diversity and Inclusiveness"; and "Times of Change or Times of Crisis?" (http://www .tristaharris.org)

Volunteer Match is a popular Internet volunteer-recruiting tool for nonprofits around the country that matches individual and workplace volunteers with thousands of nonprofit organizations. Potential volunteers can search for a nonprofit using their zip code and key words and nonprofits can register and search for volunteers with specific skills. Additionally, both volunteers and nonprofits can search for resources to help them find the best matches for their abilities and schedules. (http://www.volunteermatch.org)

White Courtesy Telephone is a hip, irreverent, and humorous site about all things third sector. Some of the posts offer links to serious articles about, for instance, training toolkits for starting up youth giving circles. Then there are the posts like one in July 2009—a letter from the White Courtesy Telephone staff to Governor Arnold Schwarzenegger offering to help restore the $144 billion in cuts the governor was making. All the governor and the California legislature need to do is grant the White Courtesy Telephone staff the power to levy taxes, they write, "a power you have but are apparently too faint of heart to exercise." The letter concludes, "We philanthropoids are many things, sir, but we are not girlie men." You get the idea. (http://www.postcards.typepad.com/white_telephone)

Other Media

Online Databases

If you are interested in research or digging deeper into an area of the nonprofit sector, or if you want to explore detailed information about nonprofit jobs or history, there are some terrific online databases to help you in your endeavor. Here is just a small sampling of what you will find.

Bureau of Labor Statistics has everything you ever wanted to know about nearly every job available in every sector, including what the future looks like for each occupation. This site is especially useful for someone interested in detailed job data and descriptions. The site also provides tutorials to help you in your search. (http://www.bls.gov)

Foundation Center has the most comprehensive database on U.S. grantmakers and grants available in the United States, according to its Web site. It also provides print, electronic, and online information resources, and publishes research on trends in foundation growth, giving, and practice. Finally, the center offers an array of free and affordable educational programs. In addition to being an online resource, the Foundation Center has several offices around the United States in Atlanta, San Francisco, Cleveland, New York, and Washington, D.C. (http://foundationcenter.org)

Indiana University-Purdue University Indianapolis Ruth Lilly Special Collections and Archives consist of the historical records of organizations and individuals that have worked as nonprofit sector advocates, philanthropists and foundations, and (mostly) Indiana-based nonprofit social service organizations. (http://www-lib.iupui.edu/special/collections/philanthropy)

National Center for Charitable Statistics at the Urban Institute is the national storehouse of data on the nonprofit sector in the United States. (http://nccs.urban.org)

Rockefeller Archive Center has everything you ever wanted to learn about philanthropic institutions. This collection includes Rockefeller family papers and the records of the various educational institutions initiated by the Rockefeller family, including Rockefeller University and the Rockefeller Foundation. (http://www.rockarch.org)

Educational Institutions

The number of universities offering programs in nonprofit management and public policy has grown exponentially over the past thirty years. Below is just a small sampling of some of the programs found throughout the United States. Keep in mind that many of these programs offer night classes for nonprofit professionals working part or full time, as well as online courses that are often part of a nonprofit certification program.

Fast Facts

PONPO

Yale University in New Haven, Connecticut (http://ponpo.som.yale.edu) runs the prestigious Program on Nonprofit Organizations (PONPO) in order to "foster interdisciplinary research aimed at developing an understanding of nonprofit organizations and their role in economic and political life." For 25 years, PONPO focused on U.S. nonprofit organizations, but it is currently redirecting its attention to the study of international non-governmental organizations in the developing world.

Case Western Reserve University, Mandel Center for Nonprofit Organizations offers a Master of Nonprofit Organizations (MNO), a Certificate in Nonprofit Management (CNM), an Executive Doctor of Management, as well as dual degree programs combining the MNO or the CNM with another degree program. (http://www.case.edu/mandelcenter/grad)

Center on Philanthropy at Indiana University is, according to this center's resource-rich Web site, "the largest and most comprehensive academic center focused on philanthropy and nonprofit management. The Center pioneered the field of Philanthropic Studies and its unique approach to the study of philanthropy through the liberal arts and other academic and professional disciplines. This pioneering has continued with the establishment of the first traditional format Ph.D. in Philanthropic Studies in the fall of 2004." (http://www.philanthropy.iupui.edu/Education)

DePaul University offers a wide array of nonprofit advanced degrees and certificates, including the following:

➜ Master of Nonprofit Management: a rigorous graduate degree that offers courses to build skills in leadership, management, ethics, and advocacy.

➜ M.S. in Public Service Management with a concentration in the following nonprofit fields: Fund Raising and Philanthropy; Health Care Administration; Higher Education Administration; Metropolitan Planning and Urban Affairs; Association Management.

➜ Certificate programs in a number of areas, including Nonprofit Management and Administrative Foundations. (http://las.depaul.edu/sps/Programs/Degrees/MasterInNonprofit-Management.asp)

Seton Hall University, Department of Public and Health care Administration offers a Master in Public Administration (M.P.A.), and graduate certificates in health care administration and nonprofit management. Students working toward the M.P.A. choose one of three concentrations: government and leadership, nonprofit management, or health policy and management. The graduate certificate in nonprofit management requires the nonprofit professional to take five classes total in such subjects as Foundations of the Nonprofit Sector, Leadership and Management of Nonprofit Organizations, Nonprofit Policy Issues: Advocacy

& Lobbying, and Managing Volunteers in Nonprofit Organizations. (http://www.shu.edu/academics/artsci/public-health care-administration/index.cfm)

University of San Diego, Institute for Nonprofit Education and Research is part of the university's Department of Leadership Studies and offers an M.A. in Nonprofit Leadership and Management and a Ph.D. in Leadership Studies with a specialization in Nonprofit/Philanthropic Leadership and Management. (http://www.sandiego.edu/soles/centers/nonprofit)

University of San Francisco, Institute for Nonprofit Organization Management offers both a master's in Nonprofit Administration and a bachelor's in Public Administration/Nonprofit Administration. (http://www.inom.org/ed/index.html)

Index